HEAL YOUR LIFE

ONE LEAF AT A TIME

ONE LEAF FOR FAITH, THE SECOND FOR
HOPE, THE THIRD FOR LOVE,
THE FOURTH FOR LUCK

BY SARA SHAW

Trilogy Christian Publishers

A Wholly Owned Subsidiary of Trinity Broadcasting Network

2442 Michelle Drive

Tustin, CA 92780

10 9 8 7 6 5 4 3 2 1

Library of Congress Cataloging-in-Publication Data is available.

ISBN 979-8-89333-205-6

ISBN 979-8-89333-206-3 (ebook)

DEDICATION

I dedicate this book to all the men, women, young and old, who for unselfish reasons shared about parts of their life. For some the journey was dark and dangerous. The hope is that their sharing may help others.

Tyra,
Sometimes helping to make a difference is just listening & caring.

Sara Shaw

ACKNOWLEDGMENTS

I ask myself where I would be without the amazing people I am blessed to know and have in my life. My family, friends, business associates, and others. Some of these friendships and relationships have spanned more than sixty years. I know I would not have finished this book without the love, encouragement, and support that I was given.

Shortly after I started interviewing to author this book about the true-life healing stories and journeys shared inside these pages, my path was abruptly interrupted. The interruption was an unintended but unfortunate situation by someone who upset the entire course and momentum of this journey. For a time, I lost my hope and my desire to continue down this path. A door had closed on me. Slowly, over several months, the encouragement, love, and prayers that surrounded me from so many people helped me remember my reasons for starting down this path. A good friend reminded me that things happen for a reason.

I was reminded about the importance of the pages and chapters that would give hope and healing to others. Chapter by chapter, story after story, I grew stronger, and I regained my passion to finish what I had started.

Thank you to my friend Sharon. You amaze me for all that you are and all that you do. You inspire me to want to do more. Thank you for your support. You are always there to help pick me up when I doubt my direction. Together, we are making a difference.

Thank you to my friend Michelle. Thank you for your guidance, your friendship, and your thoughtfulness in helping me to make some important decisions. I am most grateful.

A special thank you to some special friends and people in my life—Lorraine, Rhonda, Kris, Lisa, Kay, Mark, Cindy, Paula, Mike, Randy, Rita, Carol, Les, Bonnie, Michael, Kathy, Caryl, Zach, Joan, Carla, Barry, Martha, Brenda, Gina, Kim, Barbara, Jan, Tina, Joanne, Linda, Tony, Darlene, Rebecca, Donna, Colleen, Harriett.

A special thank you to my cousins, who are a special inspiration. Each of you deeply inspires me to be a better person.

Thank you to my mother and grandmother, whom I will forever love. I feel your presence always, from heaven.

Thank you to my husband, my children, their spouses, and my grandchildren. Your love and support warm my heart. But what warms my heart even more and makes me proud is each of you and your amazing accomplishments. Love you!

CONTENTS

CONTENTS

Website: www.sarashaw.org

Social media: X (formerly Twitter) @sarashaworg

PREFACE

After publishing my first book, *Two Sisters and The Four-Leaf Clover,* there seemed to be a lingering, a gnawing, and a push from others that there was still more to tell. There was more to be said, and that book should not be the end of the journey because it was not.

But with the first book, I never had honestly expected that it would even be published. Nor did I expect that others, after reading the book, would write personal reviews recommending it to others. Some compared it to their own life. In fact, for several months after the book was published, I still had not told some of my closest friends. My reason for this was that the truth and what I learned about my cousin's life were shocking. We had lived apart for most of our lives, so I was not prepared for what I learned. I felt it was important to protect everyone's identity because of the sexual, physical, and verbal abuse they suffered.

When I started the project, I did not know much about my cousins. But after my mother died, I felt an urge and a tugging to connect with them. Our connection was an awakening and my writing their story seemed like this was something I was supposed to do. I decided to follow my instincts. I believe the mission was heaven-sent.

I interviewed each of my cousins and wrote about the evil, cruel, and hard life they had lived. Things they suffered that I never knew about. For me, this book's purpose and importance was to give my cousins a voice. It allowed them to tell their story to help with their healing. But at the same time, being careful not to expose them and without exposing myself. The truth about what had happened had been kept secret and locked behind closed doors.

It soon became clear after the Book Reviews started coming in that this story was touching many lives. The reviews were saying that these children, my cousins who were now adults and who were hiding in shame, should not hide anymore. They were victims; they were just helpless children. The reviews shared so much compassion that my cousins started feeling safer and started coming out from their quiet places. Slowly, they were opening up about their life. As time went on, they started sharing increasingly more about their life, always with the sincere hope that they could be an inspiration and help others by doing so. For them, it was never about pity. Right from the very beginning, their identity was concealed, so their motive could not be about pity or gaining attention. We were careful about that.

Readers of the book who had also suffered started coming forward and speaking out. Some of them suffered abuse, depression, sickness, addictions, deaths, divorce, accidents, the effects of war, and many other painful hurts in their life. They wanted to have their voices heard. They, too, wanted to have a sense of relief, some understanding and acceptance. And so, it began. One by one, they told their stories. This book shares some of those true-life stories.

These pages bring to light their life journey and to where they are now. Many have deep scars and hurts. Many have also found happiness and some peace. They are not without hope, and they know they are not alone. There is a tremendous healing power in using your voice and committing it to paper to tell your story.

INTRODUCTION

So why is a four-leaf clover considered to be lucky?

A four-leaf clover has been a symbol of good luck from ancient times, maybe even going back to the very beginning of time. There are several different sources and stories to choose from that shed some light on this. Stories that make it seem possible that there truly is something extra special about a clover that has four leaves. A four-leaf clover has special meaning and value because it is rare.

One legend that is recorded shares that when Adam and Eve were being cast out of the Garden of Eden, as Eve was leaving the garden, she plucked off a single four-leaf clover to take with her. She wanted it as a souvenir of the paradise they had to leave because they had sinned. This legend about the garden, the clover, and Adam and Eve gives us a religious connection to the four-leaf clover.

The Celts were an ancient culture that once extended beyond the British Isles. Their territory stretched from Spain to the Black Sea, and geographically, they were the largest group of people to inhabit ancient Europe. The Celts thought four-leaf clovers had magical powers and would provide protection and ward off evil and bad luck. They believed four-leaf clovers provided protection from the evil fairies that tried to steal their children.

Early Egyptians thought these special clovers were very significant and valuable, too, so they gave newlyweds a four-leaf clover as a wedding gift to bless their marriage.

The Irish adopted the belief that the four-leaf clover was lucky because four-leaf clovers are much more abundant in Ireland than in comparison to other countries. Or so that is what the people who report on things like this have to say. To the Irish, their having an abundance meant that four-leaf clovers had to be lucky. Thus, "the luck of the Irish" is what we hear about the most and the symbol of a four-leaf clover is what we associate it with.

But something else that makes a lot of sense is that just finding a four-leaf clover is rare. It is well known that most stems of clover have only three leaves. Plain and simple, it is not easy to find a four-leaf clover. Even if you are searching in a large field of clover. So, if you do find one, it is easy to take the leap and conclude that you are lucky, and it will bring you *good luck*.

So why is there such a special connection and significance to the four-leaf clover for this book? Well, if you read my first book, *Two Sisters and The Four-Leaf Clover*, and turn to chapter five, you will know. There was a special meaning found on the pages of this true-life story. A story that will capture your heart and it will leave you with some lasting memories about what they suffered and endured.

But for this book, the four-leaf clover symbolizes *healing our lives* and doing it one leaf at a time using faith, hope, love, and luck to do it. Inside each of these chapters are some very special and personal true-life stories as told by many different people. You will be drawn into each of their lives, wanting to read on, needing to know how they survived it. What did they learn? Where are they now?

Over the years, we have seen beautiful illustrations in leading publications of what life was supposed to look like. Publications like the *Saturday Evening Post, Time Magazine, Newsweek*, and more. We looked at pictures and paintings of what the perfect family looked like. We watched programs and looked forward to episodes on TV of our favorite families like *Ozzie and Harriett, Father Knows Best, My Three Sons*, and others. We hoped and dreamed about having a life like the ones that we were watching. I know, for me, I always loved *Father Knows Best*. I wanted to be Kathy sitting on her dad's lap and getting hugs and reassurance. However, unfortunately, those family life dramas rarely portray what life is really like for many people.

The meaning of "keeping things behind closed doors" is to keep things hidden or kept secret from the public or without an audience or a crowd watching. There are a lot of good reasons for keeping things hidden and behind a closed door. This book is not a tell-all or a way to expose others. It is a collection of true-life stories shared for all the right reasons. Each chapter opens the door to talk about what was on the other side, hoping that these stories will bring hope and healing to others.

Healing your life—one leaf at a time.

CHAPTER ONE:

I WONDER WHAT LIFE IS LIKE FOR OTHERS

MARIE K'S INTERVIEW AND STORY.

I wonder what life is like for other people who have never suffered child or domestic abuse. I wonder what life is like for people who have not had a near-death experience, maybe from a car accident. Or those who have not had a life-threatening health scare because of a cancer diagnosis or another terminal illness. I wonder what life is like for someone who hasn't had to live their life with a disability, deaf, blind, crippled, and challenged. I wonder a lot about what life is like for other people who have had what one might call a normal life. Or at least a reasonably happy life.

For those people with a reasonably happy life, what is their morning like when they first wake up? What is the first thing they think of when they throw the covers off and open their eyes? What is their evening like when it begins to get dark outside, and the darkness of the night is all around them? Do they have any fears that come to the surface seemingly out of nowhere after the sun sets, knowing that this means that darkness follows? Do they dread falling asleep because that is when their nightmares begin?

What are the happiness triggers that pump positive dopamine

hormones directly into their brain? Like having great memories and happy smiles whenever they see bright sunshine and blue skies. When they see a field of beautiful flowers or smell something good. Like cookies baking in the oven. Or have memories of fun times going to the zoo or the park. Did they love going to school and then bringing their friends back to their house after school, spending time playing records, watching TV, and doing homework together? Did they have lots of friends?

My childhood memories are mostly sad and vague. Those are the memories that I can truly remember. For the most part, it seems that I have blocked out much of my childhood. I only have very small snippets of memories of myself with a smiling face and feeling happy. There aren't many photographs of my childhood either. And none of the smiles or feelings of happiness are memories that I have from my childhood home and living with my parents. My only memories of myself as a child when I am smiling and happy are times when I was not at my house. The good times were when I was visiting my grandmother's, my aunt's, or a friend's house.

Although I do have a memory that plays like a broken record that I cannot erase, I have a reoccurring dream, or rather, a nightmare, of myself running down the street in front of our house and being chased by my dad. He is waving his belt in the air, and I just can't seem to run fast enough to escape the beating he intends to give me. I repeat this dream over and over, and I never can get myself away and to safety. I never outrun him. He always catches me, and then he begins to beat me with his belt. In this dream, he always runs faster than I can, no matter how hard I try, then he grabs me by my clothes or by my hair, and he begins to beat me until I am left limp on the ground. Suddenly, I wake up, and I am breathing hard, gasping for air, sweating through my pajamas, and I am absolutely terrified. The funny thing about this dream is I never know what I did wrong and why he is even chasing me in the first place. I never know in this continuing nightmare what I could have possibly done wrong that would deserve such an intense determination for him to chase me down to beat me. I'm just a young girl in this dream. Maybe nine or ten years old. What could I have possibly done that is so wrong?

My flashbacks and trigger points are many, and they are all painfully emotionally consuming. They call this PTSD. Post-traumatic stress disorder. We know and often hear that many active military and veterans suffer from this, too. No doubt, many of their lives were in constant danger. The anxiety and fear that I have entirely consume me. The *trauma triggers* that set this off might be a sound that I hear, like someone yelling or screaming. That terrifies me. Or maybe it is something physical that I witness, like a push or a shove, a punch, or even a mad and mean facial expression. It is overwhelming as the anxiety and nervousness begin to wash over me. I am instantly propelled into a state of uncontrollable fear and shaking. Or I could just may-be be watching something on TV, and in the program or movie, someone is attacked, chased, stalked, or treated badly. It could be a news story about someone being hurt, abused, beaten, or killed.

I might see a child screaming and crying in a store and being hit by a parent or an adult, and at that very moment, I can't find the exit for the door fast enough to run away. I am terrified of what the outcome might be. And yet, at the same time, I want to help, but I can't. I am so terrified that I panic and then quickly walk away; I must get myself out of there. I feel weak, helpless, and afraid. I'll see a child in a restaurant that looks thin and badly dressed, and maybe they are looking down at the floor because they know they are not allowed to make eye contact. They know they are not to be heard or seen. Or a child who is outside in the cold without a warm coat or a hat and gloves for the winter. Tears flood my eyes. *Please, dear God*, I pray, *please help them*. I want to gather all the children up and take them away to safety and away from the nightmare they are living in.

It is exhausting. What I long for is to wake up just one day in my life and feel good about myself. To feel that I deserve to be happy. Some days, I linger longer in bed, hoping it will help. So many years have gone by, and for so many of those days in my past, they tip the scale towards a life weighted down with unhappiness and unworthiness.

What I long for is this feeling of unworthiness and not ever measuring up to be done and out of my life forever. For the self-loathing to stop. So many years wasted feeling sad and undeserving. Never felt loved and approved of as a child. So many beatings and tongue lashings that cause you to feel ashamed and worthless.

I long for one day to wake up and be able to say that I love myself and I approve of myself. I have said it, but I have never truly believed it. I feel like I am longing for something that is truly not possible for me, no matter how much good I do to help others and no matter how hard I strive to do my best. The emotional scars are never healed, no matter how much therapy and reassurance you are given. There isn't a pill that fixes it; it only masks the feelings, and it makes you feel numb until it is time to take another pill.

But for me, to know this and openly admit this about myself is important. It is important for others, too. Don't hide. Don't shut yourself off. Fight for yourself. Sharing the ugly, raw truth and emotions helps you, and it helps others who have suffered or who are still suffering. It helps both to know that you are not alone and that you understand what this truly feels like.

Sadly, more than a few times in my life, people whom I have trusted and confided in have stabbed me in the back. Some lied about me, and some even stole from me. And I know I am not alone in this. Many others have been treated this way, too. I am always caught off guard. I honestly do not see the benefit in trying to hurt someone else or to try to make them look bad. I think it is very important to treat others how you want to be treated. But people who are greedy and hateful can easily justify their reasons for doing what they do, and when people hurt others who are already fragile because they have lived through and suffered abuse, the impact of this crushes their spirit. They are already suffering from low self-esteem and trauma from their past. Most of them are not strong enough to be able to just shake it off. Most of them take it to heart and carry it with them. And some, they take it to heart and feel that they must have somehow deserved what happened and brought it on to themselves. That's because they lived their whole lives hearing exactly that. That "you brought this on yourself!" Another dose of hurt and pain has just been inflicted and then mentally stored.

For those people who can pick themselves back up, one would think others would be happy for them. You would hope they would look at what they had overcome and all that they have been through. But sadly, that is not always the case either. Many times, jealousy and envy show up. Some people like it best when you are down.

We have to try our best to ignore the critics and the crushers because we don't need their approval. But dear God, sometimes the critic's voice is the loudest voice in the room and in your head. You can't shake it. You can't turn down the volume.

So, I say to myself, *Try to focus on all that you have weathered.* You have lived through some very tough storms growing up. You suffered physical and emotional abuse, and you survived it. You have a voice, you have experience, you are stronger than you think. Yes, you have scars and high anxiety, and, most times, low self-esteem, but you are so much further ahead than someone who has not suffered things like this in their life. Those who have not lived through a life like yours are simply not prepared. They are not as strong as you are. At the first sign of something traumatic happening in their life, they will struggle with not knowing how to get through it. But those of us who have lived through some very rough waters know, and we can say, "I have made it this far, and I have suffered much, but I know that this, too, will pass." Find the strength that you know that you have because you have been here so many times before. Have faith and hope.

I would still like to know what it is like for others in their thoughts and their feelings when they first wake up and when they go to bed. I sincerely hope they wake up happy, and I sincerely hope they go to sleep happy, too.

For all the things that have happened in our past, our past mistakes, people who have hurt us, and other baggage that we drag around with us, we need to know whatever it was that happened, we are not damaged goods. We need to find our inner light, and we need to follow it.

Tomorrow is always a new day and a fresh start, and you deserve better.

Chapter Two:

Limb Onset ALS—The Diagnosis He Never Expected

KAY'S INTERVIEW AND STORY.

My contribution and chapter for this book is about what you do when life hurls a life-threatening, no-hope death diagnosis at you. How does this chapter compare to some of the other chapters you will read in this book? Most of the other chapters are about overcoming and healing from abuse, divorce, war, prison, abandonment, drugs, and more. All the chapters are about real life and some of the desperate hours, days, and years we fight through, hoping to be able to survive. My husband Bob fought back hard every single day to beat the odds. He chose not to give in or give up. He was not healing from his past; he was praying for healing for his future.

My hope is that his story shares that everything that we suffer in life leaves a scar and a memory, but it is never hopeless. When he left this world, his prayer was that sharing his journey might give hope to others to not ever give up. No matter what the diagnosis is or the situation you are in or something that you have suffered from that makes you think you can't overcome it. Speak up, reach out, and have faith. Together, we are stronger.

Our story is about faith, courage, and determination to

change Bob's prognosis of having only six months to two years to live.

Imagine all the emotions you would have upon hearing your diagnosis from your doctor that you have ALS, and you are being told that you need to go home and get your affairs in order. The next words you hear are, "Bob, you have six months to two years to live."

Bob had open heart surgery on November 7, 2016, at Cleveland Clinic because he had an aneurysm that was large enough that it could have ruptured at any time. He successfully had that surgery. But then, in February of 2017, Bob began having what was referred to as drop foot. Drop foot is a sign of an underlying neurological, muscular, or anatomical problem. It began for him after a hiking injury. While on vacation in Arizona, we decided to hike up to some Indian caverns. At the top of those caverns, Bob lost his footing, which caused him to twist and badly sprain his ankle. This injury is what began a long road of many possible reasons for the cause of his having drop foot. Doctors thought at first it was his knees. He was fitted with leg braces and more. Next, they thought it could be his back. He had shots and more testing, and it was determined that he needed to have back surgery. As a follow-up to surgery, he would need physical therapy, and then after therapy, more tests were ordered. Eventually, they ruled out MS and multiple sclerosis. This duration of time was over eighteen months. Eighteen long months of surgeries and treatments, and all of this had not helped. Being frustrated and concerned, we discussed and decided to make an appointment at the Cleveland Clinic. Within the first thirty minutes of our appointment at Cleveland Clinic in August of 2018, Bob was sadly diagnosed with Limb Onset ALS and given the diagnosis of six months to two years to live.

ALS stands for amyotrophic lateral sclerosis. It even sounds scary. ALS is often called Lou Gehrig's disease. Lou Gehrig was a famous baseball player who suffered and died from ALS. It is a rare and terminal neurodegenerative disease that results in the progressive loss of motor neurons that control all your voluntary muscles.

Bob began speaking carefully, slightly slurring because the disease was already affecting his speech. ALS is relentless, and it affects every part of your nervous system. It affects the nerve cells in your brain and your spinal cord, which then causes a complete loss of muscle control. The progression of ALS affects all the muscles that have control over your ability to move, walk, talk, dress and feed yourself, swallow, and even breathe. He was told by the doctors that there was no cure. The prognosis that he was given was that it was hopeless. What a terrible, frightening picture and a description of what it was going to be like for the progression and suffering that he would have. He was told he should be prepared for six months with hope for longer.

In our home, it was our turn to host our prayer group. With all of us sitting together in our living room, both Bob and I shared with each of them that our faith in God was much bigger and stronger than our fear of the diagnosis. Our group knew how strong our faith was and they believed this, too. We said to them, "We are going to put this in God's hands and ask for all the things that we need to do to beat this." Our faith was so strong that many others also believed that we could change the course and outcome. We carried with us in our hearts and on our lips the verse from Matthew 19:26 (NIV): "With God all things are possible."

From the very day that we were told the diagnosis, we were determined to fight it. We immediately began researching as best we could to find others who had this disease. What were they doing? We researched to find doctors, providers, and other professionals who were getting some positive and reliable results. What were others doing to help, change, and delay this terrible diagnosis? And while we were on this journey, whatever we learned we would share to help others. Together, we believed, and it became our mission to look for a cure and to pray and believe that it was possible. Our believing, our never doubting and having faith were our strengths. We were dedicated to getting through this together. No matter what it took.

Bob and I were high school sweethearts. He was fifteen and I was sixteen when we started dating, and as the story goes, I handpicked him to be my boyfriend and my husband. He was cute and good at football and basketball. He was polite and the perfect gentleman. He was such a perfect gentleman that after several dates without him giving me a kiss goodnight at my doorstep, one night, I took matters into my own hands. I decided it was time for our first kiss, so I made the move. I pulled him by his shirt while we were standing on my porch, and then I kissed him. It felt like we were meant to be together. We continued dating, and when Bob was twenty-one and I was twenty-two, we were married. We remained together and married for fifty-three years. We had one son, a daughter, and five grandchildren.

Bob died at the age of seventy-four. We were blessed that he lived two years longer than the awful "only six months to two years to live" diagnosis that he was given. There was not a day that went by that he ever gave up hope or lost his faith. It was not because it was not hard, because it was extremely hard. He struggled through it and stayed positive even as he had to use his BiPap ventilator just to be able to breathe. His attitude was "to never give up." I don't know how he was able to fight on like he did. He was so brave and so strong, and I deeply admired this dear and special man that I loved so much.

His faithfulness to God started in his childhood. Bob had twelve bars or pins from his church, which meant that he had never missed a Sunday church service, starting from the first grade through the twelfth grade. While we were dating, we never stayed out late on a Saturday night because of church the next day on Sunday.

Bob always lived a healthy lifestyle. He never smoked. He was a light drinker, he did not eat sweets, and he ate a healthy diet. He jogged, and he did two hundred push-ups every morning for most of his life.

For a big part of his work career, he was in IT. With his strong computer skills, he was easily able to begin his research on special treatments that were going on across the country for ALS. Again, it was important to him that all this knowledge that he would gain from his research he could then document so that he could use it to help others.

From his research, there were several changes that he made to his daily living with me right by his side for whatever it was that he needed. The following are some of the ALS treatments, professionals, and therapies that he used and wanted to share.

Dr. Richard Bedlack is currently a Professor of Neurology at Duke and the Director of the Duke ALS Clinic is the leader of the international ALS Untangled program, which utilizes social networks to investigate alternative treatment options. He also leads the ALS Reversals program which attempts to understand why some people do recover from ALS. Dr. Bedlack cited fifty-five cures. Cures mean there is hope. Cure means to have faith.

Peptides were another choice he used as a potential therapeutic target. They were administered under the care of a neurologist. To better understand, one would have to research and inquire about neurotrophins and neuroprotective peptides. To understand this is not easy, but this treatment was specific to treating neurodegenerative diseases.

Hyperbaric oxygen therapy (HBOT) is administered through a hood in a multi-place chamber. Length of treatment time and pressure varied. Treatments were sixty to ninety minutes each and given once or twice a day. The treatment helps with tissues that are low in oxygen, which affects healing. This treatment has also been referred to as healing under pressure. Bob did over forty dives. Bob told me he thought he felt the best with these treatments.

We were extremely encouraged by Kim Cherry's website, ALS Winners – The Road to Recovery. His own story provides much hope. He was first diagnosed with ALS on November 22, 2011, and he was told that he had a year to live. Kim is alive and well, playing golf, traveling, and enjoying his life at the time of writing down this information, which is September 2022. Kim was a true inspiration. We listened, learned, and followed through on the changes and recommendations he gave. We traveled to attend the healing conference that was held in Salt Lake City, Utah, which is held every other year. This is the website: www.healingalsconference.org.

The conference speakers were resolute ALS professionals and fellow allies of ALS. It was so encouraging to hear and see the groups of people who had successfully reversed their disease. There was *hope*, and that hope was filling the room. The day the conference ended, we left filled with hope, encouragement, and a new determination. The months that Bob lived past his diagnosis, we believe, were because of the dedicated and prayerful approach and the many professionals and allies we followed and stayed connected with during his journey.

The following are some of those changes that helped to make a difference.

It is important to go barefoot. Our feet need to be touching the ground to be able to draw in natural healing energy. This is called grounding.

Bob had all his mercury fillings removed. My career was in dentistry, so this was a revelation for both of us for sure. It was explained to us that mercury is found in amalgam fillings. Bob had his mercury fillings removed by a special biological dentist to be sure they were removed safely and to prevent the possibility of additional contamination.

I worked tirelessly to prepare for him special nutritionally recommended meals to help promote his healing. I boiled bones for the collagen to make him broth. I shopped for only fresh organic food choices. We eliminated all sugar, gluten, and dairy. We researched the vitamin supplements recommended by Kim Cherry, and Bob faithfully followed this strict diet and vitamin regimen. We were never deviating from it.

We believed that all this was making a positive difference. We had many of our friends praying and believing and supporting us every step of the way in all that we were doing.

The following message can be found on Kim Cherry's website:

You must believe you can get well. We did it, and so can you too. One interesting thing I learned quite recently is that your mind controls your body. Your brain controls every function in your body. So, use your brain to be positive, to believe that you can get better. Your cells listen to your thoughts and speech. Ask the Lord for his help. Then go to work to give your body its best chance possible to heal. Our protocol included hyperbaric, ozone, proper nutrition, exercise, supplements, and avoidance of as many toxins as possible.

When I reflect on all the changes we made and the treatments I believe that we did everything we could do. Together, Bob and I never gave up or lost hope. Not until we felt that God was calling Bob home.

I deeply miss him; we had been together as a couple for such a long time. I was sixteen years old when we started dating. To-day, I am seventy-six. We spent fifty-nine years together. The sweet and loving memories I have of him will always be with me. We were blessed with a close and beautiful family and the loving support of many dear friends. Together, we set the bar high for ourselves for trying to be good people and good Chris-tians. We had a beautiful life together. I always said that I had picked him. But he would always say, "No, I picked you."

While Bob was undergoing some medical care at the Univer-sity of Michigan hospital, he was told that medical research and data had proven that the area of lower Michigan and Northern Ohio in the Lake Erie region had been found to have the highest number of ALS cases. We both lived in the region. But he was also exposed to other environmental factors from the surrounding farming area and working in the construction business with his father. Usually, ALS strikes people at a much younger age. I shared my thoughts about this with Bob. I attributed his delay and onset until later in his life was most likely because of his healthy lifestyle.

ALS is a terrible disease. Through it all, Bob's strength, courage, and devotion were such an inspiration. He showed us what the love of God and having faith can get you through. He showed such courage and bravery because of his strong faith. He inspired many others to find God and to never give up until that final day when God calls you home.

Our prayer for others is no matter what you are dealing with in your life, have faith and have hope. Try your best to defy the odds until God calls you home.

Chapter Three:

She Did What She Had to Do—But Her Children Paid the Price for It

NANCY'S INTERVIEW AND STORY.

Because of my childhood trauma that was caused by suffering years of sexual, physical, and verbal abuse by my stepfather for most of my adult life, I have secluded myself from others. I feel the need to protect myself, and I have a lot of reasons for doing so. My not being able to trust other people is a significantly concerning factor in my life. A parent is supposed to love you, protect you, and guide you. Growing up without that protection and security makes it exceedingly difficult to feel like you can trust anyone. I never felt safe as a child, and I was not alone in that. I also heard and saw my siblings and my mother suffer day after day after day. It was a never-ending nightmare for all of us. And no one ever came to our rescue, to save us. Because of that, I have deep resentment for some relatives and others. In my heart, I think some members of our family could have helped, but instead, they distanced themselves from the situation.

I know that there were a few attempts of help, like by my real father, but the fear of death that my stepfather threatened on anyone who interfered stopped the possibility of our escaping the nightmare that we suffered. Even the authorities were not able to protect us. If social services showed up because of being alerted or suspicious because of bruises, black eyes, and more, we were all threatened by him that if we told the truth about what was happening, we would all pay big for it, and we would never see each other ever again. His words, "Paying big for it"…we all had suffered and had witnessed what "paying big for it" looked like and what it felt like many times before. There were times in our life when you were beaten so badly that you felt sure that this was the time that you were not going to live through it.

I also have emotional baggage that has a powerful control over me. Sometimes, it is overwhelmingly consuming. I feel so much shame, guilt, and fear. I stop myself and say, wait a minute, why do I feel shame? I was the victim, not the perpetrator. Why do I feel shame and guilt? But I do; it is inside of me like a disease.

I do understand the fear and shame that I have. It is because of the conditioning and control an abuser has over you. Every day, you are made to feel stupid and unworthy. You are made to feel that everything about you is bad. You are told that you do not have any good qualities at all. You are worthless. You can't do anything right, and you deserve every bad thing that happens to you. It is all your own fault. You have brought all this on yourself.

I wonder how many others suffer and relate to this. It is exhausting.

Yes, this is conditioning and control. I want to emphasize this and share because this is how young people fall prey to human trafficking, drug addiction, suicide, and other life-threatening outcomes. The perpetrators first lure you into thinking this is all going to be something wonderful. Soon after, when they have conditioned you, you are then well on your way to being thrown into the pits of hell, and they have complete control over you.

Along the path of my life as an adult, little by little, I started to feel brave enough to open my closed door, but just a tiny bit. I started to peek out from behind my door, which concealed my dark secrets from others. My very private, safe place. But I knew I would not dare want others to know about my shameful past. Not only would they look down on me, they would not want to associate with me either. I knew this to be true because I was told repeatedly by my stepfather that I was dirty, shameful, and dis-gusting. I felt others would look down on me and talk about me behind my back. When I was out and about, I did not know who might know things about me. This would then make me feel like everybody knew something and was talking about me. I was par-anoid. It feels like I have a tattoo on my forehead that marks and identifies me to others that I am a shameful person.

I am incredibly sad that some people relish diminishing and hurting other people. Some gossipers are even churchgoers. Maybe they cannot help themselves. Maybe they are what is re-ferred to as "a work in progress." I feel when someone like that has a chance to make someone else look bad, perhaps they do so because it makes them feel better about themselves. But for myself, I already struggle with my self-worth, so being judged and talked about just diminishes me and reinforces my feelings of mistrustfulness.

I am incredibly careful about the things I say about others. I don't want to cause others pain. Whenever I would start to think it was okay to open my door to let others in, a shushing finger in front of my lips would appear. That image was telling me to only open the door just a tiny crack. It is still not safe out there; be very careful. You do not know who to trust.

But leaving my door open a tiny crack allowed me to begin to meet and get to know and even begin to trust a few special people. These special people, I believe, were heaven-sent. These were extra-special people because as we got to know each other, they did not see me at all as shameful and dirty. The more they listened and learned, the more compassion and genuine closeness we felt. And many of those people had their secrets and they were grateful to be able to talk out loud about their lives as well. We were supportive of each other. Sharing our secrets became our medicine. Now that special medicine is helping others. So many of us have baggage, hurts, and issues.

When I turned eighteen, I followed through with my plan to leave home and move miles and miles away. I remember that day. I could finally declare, "I am free." Yes, I left my mother and siblings behind, and because of that, I hurt deeply, but I knew that their day to escape from hell would come for them, too. I also feel strongly, even years later, that if I had not left, I would have probably become a prostitute for sexual favors. I had been conditioned by my stepfather and told that prostitution was my only and best option.

I desperately wanted a better life, and I had a lot that I had to try and deal with, knowing now that I was safely away from all the abuse. One of the things that always troubled me was my not understanding how a mother could let this happen to her children. Why did she keep us in an abusive and dangerous relationship? I knew my stepfather threatened her with death, losing her kids, and all sorts of terrible threats. But I must be honest, I still question this. I know I would have handled it differently, and some way and somehow, I would have protected my children. My mother always said that I was the sassy one. I would have done more.

My mom passed away several years ago now, and I know that I loved my mom, and I am not trying to make her look bad. I am just saying that for me, the way that I think and the way that I feel about my child and my grandchild, I would never have let them go through what I did. I am baring my soul and being most honest and truthful. It does not make me a bad daughter or my mother a bad mother. I know she said she did what she thought she had to do. However, she was not able to be a good role model because of the choices that she felt she had to make. This became even more apparent to me when I gave birth to my first child. When I became a mother, it reinforced for me what I always thought and felt, and that was that when I grew up and became a mother, I would forever protect this most precious gift from God. I would also work hard to provide and give this child all the things that I never had. I can tell you I did all that and even more. I went overboard because of it.

There are many things that I am left with not being able to understand about my mother and why she did what she did. My horrible past and memories show up in my thinking some days completely uninvited, and then they completely consume my consciousness. The conversations I have with myself never conclude and end with my not loving my mother. It is not about forgiveness either. I know unforgiveness is the poison you drink, so I am always about forgiveness. But I am angry. I do not mean hateful anger; I am careful about that, too. I just feel mad. I am angry because of the loss of my childhood, and I'm resentful that my childhood was a prison camp where we suffered daily beatings, terror, sexual abuse, and demeaning and hateful verbal abuse. I am mad, I am angry, and then I start to cry. Why, Mom? Why? How could you let this happen? Why did it have to be this way? I am sorry, but I think there was something that you could have done. We were just helpless children.

I do not like knowing or admitting where I came from. But the good thing that came out of it is it drove me to work harder at everything that I have ever attempted. I would be better, and I would gain respect. I can honestly say that I am happy with myself for what I have accomplished. Along the way, it was always a bonus for me to receive any kind of acknowledgment or admiration for my accomplishments. Sadly, I do not have any memory of ever hearing as a child the words "good job," "well done," or "we are proud of you."

Still, to this day, I do not feel I will ever be able to say that I am healed. At least now, because of my sharing about the awful parts of my life and talking out loud about it, I have received some healing. I have some relief. But the face that I still see in the mirror never gets my approval.

After myself and my siblings had all left home, our mother continued to live and stay with my stepfather until he died. I often wish I would have asked her before she died why she stayed. Did she still feel trapped? Did she think it would be better with the kids gone? Or was it because by the age she was then, she was so tired and hopeless she just did not care anymore? How did our mother feel about her life? What were her demons? What did she see when she looked in the mirror?

I know that I am a very aware person. What I mean by that is I can sense, when I am around other people, those who are giving off good energy and those who are not. I can see a child across the room who has a good home life and one that probably does not. I am extremely sensitive to others who I sense are suffering. I pray for them.

I am still in the process of figuring out my purpose in life. I am feeling better about who I am, but I am not completely accepting of myself. The years are passing me by, and I so desperately want to be more, achieve more, love more, have more respect for myself, and have some peace of mind. I ask myself, "What will it take?" I think it starts with being honest about who you are now and what you have been through. To know it was not your fault and to know you truly do deserve better. You deserve to be happy. Stop playing the old movies in your mind that keep you from having and thinking you deserve your self-approval.

Life is a risk. You could be here today and gone tomorrow. So, I know how important it is to get there. To find that happier place of self-acceptance. I do not want to leave this world before I can accomplish and achieve my approval. I believe in the eyes of the Lord that He sees my good. I pray that He helps me so that I, too, can see my good. He helps me to be able to help others who have suffered trauma and deserve healing and acceptance as well.

For those of you who have read about my journey, my hope for you is that it helps to bring some healing for you in your life, no matter what it is that you may have suffered.

For others and me, I hope and pray for that day when we can look at ourselves in the mirror and like that face we see.

CHAPTER FOUR:

GRIEF SHREDS YOU APART UNTIL YOU HARDLY KNOW WHO YOU ARE OR WHY YOU WOULD WANT TO GO ON

MARYANN'S INTERVIEW AND STORY.

I am seventy-seven years old. I am passionate about helping others. I was told by a friend that sharing some of my life stories because of what I have lived through could bring hope and healing for others. I pray that it will. I am passionate about helping others because I know what desperation, pain, fear, and hopelessness feel like. I have lived through all of this for most of my life. And I know what it feels like, as a mother, to lose a child. I have lost three of my children.

I was born in 1945 in West Virginia. The year I was born is a particularly important year in history because it marked the end of World War II and the fall of Nazi Germany. German concentration camps were liberated, and the Holocaust genocide of millions ended. A few months later, Japan surrendered after the United States dropped nuclear bombs on Hiroshima and Nagasaki. So much death and destruction this war brought. So, when the war ended, there was new hope for the future. History tells us that many families flourished after the war because it was the new era of modern industrialization. There were new jobs and lots of opportunities. With all this new hope, it was a good year to be born into this world. That is, unless you were born and living in West Virginia, and West Virginia is my birthplace.

In other parts of the world, post-World War II, things were booming with endless opportunities and economic expansion. But the people of Appalachia were suffering economic, social, and even environmental hardships. Many were dependent on welfare. They were trapped without employment; many suffered illness and lived without hope. Some were able to leave West Virginia for good and moved to another state.

Some of the whys for this are that West Virginia was suffering from a decline in coal use. Rugged land was not ideal for producing profitable farming. The land and mountains also hindered industrial and commercial expansion. I have a better understanding now about life for people in Appalachia, and it seems that, unfortunately, West Virginia has always struggled economically in comparison to other states.

In 1955, I was ten years old, and my mom and dad decided to move the family to Ohio. I have one sister and two brothers, and I am the oldest sibling. As the oldest, I was the full-time babysitter. Whenever my siblings did anything wrong, I was the one who took the beating from my dad. After all, it was my fault if they were being bad because I was in charge.

I never told anyone much about my life until I was fifty years old. It was my fiftieth birthday, and I asked for a family sit down. Before this day, it was just too hard even to start that conversation knowing how awful the truth was. My real father sexually abused me from the time I was ten years old until I ran away from home at age fourteen. The mean, harsh, and painful beatings that he gave me had started long before that. Those beatings and the sexual abuse continued until I finally decided I could not take it anymore, and I ran away.

Growing up in that house with all the abuse, I felt anger and fear. Other people, including relatives, thought that I had a mean streak in me. Because of this, I was always considered to be the black sheep in the family. But I wasn't a black sheep; I was a *fighter*. I had to be a fighter for survival. I acted out because I was angry about my life and what was happening to me. The abuse I suffered from my dad squeezed the joy out of my life and left me feeling nothing but anger, hurt, and resentment.

My mother was unaware for a long time. My dad played it all out so smartly. He would wait until my mother was busy outside gardening or when she would leave for out of town for a few days to visit her sister. He threatened me that I had better never tell my mother or anybody else about the sexual abuse. There would be dire consequences if I told anyone. I would take a terrible beating, one that I would not soon forget, and then I would be taken away and put into a home or a detention center.

I would stay outside of our house for hours upon hours just to be out and away from him. My going inside the house would put me at risk of my dad taking me into the bedroom for sex. If I were away at school or church, I would stay away as long as possible. I remember a pastor from church who knew something at home was not good for me, so he would invite me to visit his home after church. This helped to keep me safe for just a little while longer.

After days, months, and years of both the sexual abuse and the beatings, one day I said I was going to tell my mother. My dad grabbed me and put me in the car. As far as I knew, this ride that we were taking was going to come true to what he had threatened so many times over the years. The threat was ringing in my ears. If I told my mother, I would be taken away and put in a home. I thought that this was that ride on that day. He was taking me to the orphanage or a detention center. At some point during the ride in the car, he told me that he promised that he would not touch me or do this to me anymore. He said that he had control over this and he would not have sex with me anymore. We drove a little longer, and at some point, when he thought he had finally convinced me that it was over and I agreed that I would not tell my mother, we headed back home. I believed my dad because, after all, it was a promise. I should trust him. He was my dad. It was understood and settled, so we headed back home.

When we returned home, my mom asked us where we had gone. My dad explained that he took me for a car ride because I had a bad attitude and I needed a talking-to. I guess that to make his story look good, he then took me outside and whipped me with a switch. Again, I was the bad one.

My dad never hit my mom. And out of the four kids, he beat me the most. My mom put my dad on a pedestal. She thought he was a wonderful husband and defended and bragged about him to everyone all the time.

I did tell my mom at some point that my dad was sexually abusing me, but sadly, my mom did not believe me. She said I was lying. That left me without hope. I had no one to protect me.

I learned years back that my dad's father, who is my grand-father, sexually abused and beat his family, too. I have thought now for a long time that this was just the culture in some places in the South. You have heard about this a lot. I thought perhaps it became worse because of the hard life people had living in the Appalachians. But I am learning more and more that this happens all around the world. It happens to rich and poor people. The abuser threatens harm to the victim, and some threaten harm to the victim's family, too, if they tell anybody. So, then the victim lives in fear without any power, and they are under the complete control of the abuser.

Many people look the other way regarding family and child abuse, so the abuser gets away with it. People do not want to know or hear about it. A lot of mothers, just like my mother, nev-er believe that their husband or boyfriend is sexually and phys-ically abusing their children. And that was my life. As we have heard it said so often, it is a topic others want to sweep under the rug. It is the elephant in the room that no one wants to recognize and acknowledge.

I was fourteen years old when I ran away from home to Tennessee with my boyfriend Billy to get married. I thought Billy was the spitting image of Elvis Presley, and I was about to be his bride. No one ever asked for proof of my age to get married. That includes Billy. I had not told Billy my real age. I so desperately wanted out of the house. My marriage to Billy lasted for eighteen years. When I ran away, my mother went to work at a hospital. It was said that she did this so that she could earn money to help me.

I had escaped my father and the sexual and physical abuse I suffered living with him and my mother. But sadly, I escaped nothing. My husband Billy beat me our entire married life. We had five children. My heart still breaks when I think back because he beat our children, too. Every time I stepped in to protect our children, he beat me within an inch of my life. Billy had also grown up in an abusive home. In his situation, it was his mother who beat him. It tears me apart recalling when one of our daughters, in such desperation, thought her dad would love her more if she was a boy and he might stop beating her. So, in her attempt to please him, she cut off her hair to look more like a boy. This was all so sick and messed up.

Three of our children passed away. We had four girls and one boy.

Billy did not work much. I was the main breadwinner. My father, much to my surprise, did help us buy a house. So, there was some good in him. But even as I just shared that there was some good in him, I hesitate and want to take that back. One of our daughters has a slight memory of my dad, her grandfather, molesting her when she was a little girl. It seems very real to her but something she cannot see clearly. She feels traumatized just thinking about it. She suffers lots of health issues to this day related to all that she had to live with growing up.

I did try to shoot Billy one time. He was in a rage and threatening all of us, and he dared me to shoot him. It was one of our daughters' birthdays. I aimed the gun straight at him. He knocked the barrel down, and I just missed shooting him.

When our oldest daughter was about five years old, Billy knocked her into a glass shower door during one of his rages. She suffered broken bones, cuts, and bruises. She could have been killed.

Our beautiful four-year-old daughter was sick and dying. She was born with severe health issues, and we were told that she would probably only live to be about two years old. At age four, she was sick and in the hospital, and, at that time, I was pregnant with another child. Before my little girl died, she would smile and talk to us, saying that she was so excited because she was going to get a new baby brother. It was Easter Sunday, and she told us, "I know I am still gonna get my brother." She died shortly after Easter Sunday. Her baby brother was born on July 28. He was one month and one day old when he died. Per the hospital, it was from several health issues. My little girl got her new baby brother to meet her up in heaven. We lost another daughter to SIDS. I believe in my heart that they were better off leaving this world because they were spared from the awful beatings by Billy.

One day, I was babysitting to help earn a little extra money. Billy started hitting me and was accusing me of seeing someone else. I took a butcher knife to scare him and get him to stop. He called the police. The police had been called a few times before, but this time, the police came and arrested me, and I went to jail. Our kids went to stay with their aunt, my sister.

He tried to prove to the court that I was an unfit mother and the kids should be taken away from me. Instead, the judge for the case, after hearing all the evidence, threatened to put him in jail. Billy, after this, said he was sorry and that it would be different. I foolishly went back to him.

We had been married for eighteen years when I found out that Billy had been seeing another woman. He said he wanted to get a divorce and marry her because she had a nice house. I also figured out at some point that he had slept with my best friend and fathered a child with her that looked exactly like one of our daughters. I had tried hard to always believe that he would change. That things would get better for the children and me. My parents had drilled into me that marriage was a bond that you did not break. Till death do you part? God knows I tried.

My eighteen years of living in this horrible situation being married to Billy had finally hit rock bottom. Billy had already moved out, and he asked if he could borrow my car. One day, I was sitting in a restaurant with our children, looking out the window, when I saw him drive by the restaurant with his girlfriend in my car. I was so angry. I called my uncle and asked him to come pick up my kids. I was going to have it out with Billy. I confronted him and told him to give me my car back. He flew into a rage and started beating me, and it was one of the worst beatings ever. When my daughter saw how badly I was beaten, she came to me crying and said that if I did not leave Billy for good, that was it for her: she would be moving out. She said she would leave and go live with her aunt. That was my turning point. I could not lose my daughter. My ending of the marriage should have been years and years sooner. I know that. I was broken. I believed all the lies that things would change. I have no excuse. I was foolish.

When I divorced Billy, my father showed up in court for me. That day was the first time that my father cried and told me that he loved me. For some reason, my mother had always liked Billy. Billy was always very nice to her, and my mother did not know everything that had been going on. On the day of my divorce, my mother decided to get drunk. This was concerning and hard to believe because my mother was not a drinker. I will never forget that day. It is also worth mentioning that Billy has been married four times.

The pedestal that my mom had my dad on and all her bragging came to an end one day. It was not until my father was in the hospital dying that my sister finally told my mother that I had been molested by my dad.

It came out because my mom was complaining about the way I was. She said that I always seemed mad and mouthy. My sister answered her back and told her it was time that you knew the truth. She told our mom, "It is understandable my sister is the way she is. She was sexually molested by our dad, your husband, starting at age ten until she ran away. And he beat her all the time." My sister went on to tell my mother that our dad had molested her, too. When my sister told me what she had told our mom, this was the first time that I knew that my dad had molested my sister, too. Finally, my mother could not deny it any longer.

About a year after our father died, our mother took down all the pictures of my dad hanging on the walls in the house. She never spoke about or asked any questions about what had happened to us. She never again spoke about what a wonderful man he was either. Sadly, though, she never said she was sorry that it had all happened to us. This was our mother. Her love, comfort, understanding, and even some sympathy could have helped so much with our healing. We were broken and incredibly sad. I am sad that my mother had to suffer this.

I never turned my back on God. Early on, though, I never really got involved with the church. But these last fifteen years of my life now, I do not know what I would have done without God.

When my children died, that is when I needed God the most.

My second husband, Phil, passed away seven years ago. I met him ten years after my divorce from Billy, and I was thirty-eight years old. Phil hated Billy. He knew what a terrible human being he was. My husband Phil was a wonderful man. He was such a blessing and an answer to prayer.

When Phil was sick and dying, I prayed for him one night after he suffered a bad fall in the bathroom. Phil was six feet eight inches tall. It took all my strength to help him up. That night, I prayed, "Dear God, please take him or get me some help." The very next day, Phil passed away. I loved Phil, and I still miss him. He was so good to me. After he died, I joined a wonderful group to help with my grieving. I desperately needed this. The group is called Grief Share, and it is a national organization. Today, I am happy to say that I am one of the leaders. I know what belonging and being a part of this group did for me. I urge others who have suffered the loss of loved ones to reach out. It is hard to heal on your own. Sharing and being with others helps with the hurt and healing.

Trust is a real problem for me. It has been for most of my life. Who can you trust? It does not feel safe for me to trust. I could not even trust my father. I also could not trust or believe my first husband when he said things would change and there would be no more beatings. I still suffer flashbacks. I am very claustrophobic and even afraid in elevators. This fear is from all the times that my dad locked me in a dark closet. I would be kicking and screaming and begging for him to let me out. Some nights, I still find it hard to get to sleep just thinking about it.

What makes me feel good about myself is when I can help others. Every day is a new day, and I say to myself, it is a day that I can help make a positive difference for others. One of the ways is by being part of the leadership team at Grief Share. I have lived through so much pain and sadness that my compassion for others is sincere. I have been there. I have lived it.

My sincere hope in sharing a part of my life in my chapter of this book is that others will know that you are worthy. You can have a better life, and you deserve a better life. Don't wait, start today. Life is short, and we hear this often. So, begin now to live a better life. Believe that you can have it, deserve it, and have faith. God bless.

BELIEVE

Protect those secrets and keep them in place

Is it shame written all over your face?

Don't let it be what people greet

Don't keep staring at your feet

The pain of shame says we aren't good enough

That we're not certain we have the right stuff

We are children of God, saved by Christ

Ask for forgiveness

Do it tonight

Believe

Christ died for our sins

Believe in Him

Bonnie A. Honaker

Chapter Five:

What I Learned and Want to Share about Failed Relationships, Narcissism, and NPD

FAITH'S INTERVIEW AND STORY.

I know it to be true; she had told me enough times in my life. My mother hated me, and she was jealous of everyone I dated and the men that I married. My mother was a narcissist. She suffered from narcissistic personality disorder. NPD. Narcissism is a big word. A word, title, and definition that I didn't know much about or that I even heard about until much later in my life. Much, much later in my life, and after enduring many years of pain, abuse, and sadness. It turns out I am attracted to people who hurt me the most. I always think I can earn their love and respect. If I am a good daughter. If I am a hard worker. A good wife. If I am a good cook and our home is sparkling clean. If I cater to their every need. I always put them first and their needs and desires. I always think and do for them before me. If I do all this, I deserve their love, and they will never want to lose me. It will be important to them. And I will feel special and needed. They will love me. That is what I need the most. To feel love and be loved.

Narcissism is a self-centered personality style that is

characterized as having an excessive preoccupation with oneself and one's own needs, and in almost all cases, it is at the expense of others.

Then, there is narcissistic personality disorder or NPD.

This person looks and acts with grandiosity. Boy, do they think they are all that and

more! And they are always thinking they deserve more. They have a complete lack of empathy, care, and concern for other people. They want and expect admiration. They are arrogant, self-centered, manipulative, and demanding. They have big ideas, and they feel they deserve special treatment. They expect and demand special treatment.

I carry a list with me that details nine of the NPD traits that I learned about through therapy and research. This important list serves as a careful reminder for me. It is my red alert and beware reminder. Danger, danger! I gladly give this list to others when I feel it will help them.

This list is called "Special Me" by Duke Health:

1. Sense of self-importance

2. Preoccupation with power, beauty, or success

3. Entitled

4. Can only be around people who are important or special

5. Interpersonally exploitative for their gain

6. Arrogant

7. Lack of empathy

8. Must be admired

9. Envious of others or believe that others are envious of them.

My awakening happened when I started attending a women's abuse support group. I wish I had learned about NPD years and years earlier. The personal title I have given this personality is "the devil's spawn." In my opinion, this is a person who could easily be Satan's right-hand man.

These evil personalities groom their victims. They suck you in, suck your air out and take everything they can from you. You are left feeling worthless.

First, they draw you in, making you think you are special. And when you are completely sucked in, they beat you down until your self-worth is completely diminished.

You fall for their stories. They are manipulative. They are evil. They are—"the devil's spawn."

I was born in 1959. At the time of writing this, I am now sixty-four years old.

I have five older brothers. Four of them are either alcoholics or drug addicts. My dad was also an alcoholic, and my mother was promiscuous, mean, and a narcissist. I feel bad for my brothers because my dad beat them all the time.

I was born with a slight disability. At birth, my legs had to be broken and reset because of a muscular deformity. I still have a nerve and muscular disability.

As a kid growing up, when my dad got off work, he went right to the bar. By the time he came home, he was always drunk. His coming home and being drunk was bad news because it meant that he was going to be as mean as possible to all of us. We were all scared to death of him when he was like this, so my brothers and I all knew how to scatter, to be gone and out of sight. That meant crawling out the windows and escaping the house. Run fast and get away. And we all knew to stay away until we heard a horn honking. That horn honk would be our mother sending us the signal that it was safe to come home. The horn honk meant our dad had passed out for the night, sound asleep.

My safe haven was a neighbor's house during that time. They were a wonderful family that fed me, we prayed before dinner, and they took me to church. I learned about God. I ate green beans, even though I did not like them, but the family did, so I ate mine, too. I felt like I was part of a family. I spent summers there when my parents went missing. This is a rich and thankful memory for me, and I am so grateful for them.

One time, when I was about eight years old, I came home in the afternoon, and no one was there. Evening came, it was dark, and at 11 p.m., there was still no mom and dad. My two brothers, who still lived at home, were nowhere to be found either. I was only eight years old, and I was all alone. No notes, no calls. I was scared, and so I decided to call my oldest brother. He picked me up and took me to his house. My mom called him the next day, and she asked him if he knew where I was. He was so angry and disgusted with her. He lied and said that he did not know. Not too long ago, I asked my second oldest brother what he thought about how my life was growing up. He told me that he thought that I had pretty much raised myself on my own. Our mom and dad were not around much for me, and if they were, it was not a healthy environment. When he told me that, it reminded me that there was one whole summer when my mom was not home.

I have a recurring nightmare that my brothers and I are running down a dark hallway and jumping over dead bodies while trying to make our escape. It seems like it truly happened.

At age fourteen, I was my dad's chauffeur. Obviously, I did not have a driver's license at age fourteen. But I had to drive him to and from the beer joint and to and from his vacation trailer. I had to spend time in the beer joint, too. I didn't dare complain or ask to leave, or a heavy hand would come down on me. I remember one time my dad was drunk, and he insisted he was driving. My youngest brother and I were in the car. He tried to drive up the side of a very steep hill, and it scared us half to death as the car almost rolled over. We were screaming, we were terrified.

We moved around a lot—as an example, in seventh grade I attended seven different schools for that school year. I have horrible memories of some of the places that we lived. I also am not sure about the why and reasons for us having to move around so much.

I do have a fond memory of having my own pony as a little girl. Our neighbor at one of the places we lived at early on gave it to me; they kept it in their stables. Sometimes, I would stay out all hours of the night just riding the pony. I felt safe being outside and riding my pony.

I have a vivid memory of hiding from my dad at a gas station with my mother and my youngest brother. My memory is that my brother and I were hiding inside a car. The owner at the gas station would hoist the car up in the air on the lift to keep us from being seen in case our dad stopped by. We hid up there for hours. If we had to go to the bathroom, we would honk the horn, and the owner would hoist us down. My mother stayed in the office with the owner. Now, either we were hiding from my dad because he was drunk, or my mom was messing around with the man in the office at the gas station. I am not sure about this.

One of my brothers was hit by a car and suffered permanent disabilities. He is the brother that I was closest to.

When I was at the age of nine or ten, my mom left my dad, or he threw all of us out. I am not sure. She was sleeping around. One of her many lovers was a door-to-door sweeper salesman. Fortunately, or unfortunately, it depends on how you look at it, he owned an abandoned apartment building in a very rough part of town. An abandoned building tells you the living quality was not good. We lived in this abandoned apartment building for several months. We did not go to school during this time, and my mom was giving sexual favors to feed us. One time, I remember being in a phone booth with my mom, and some big scary man kept reaching in and stroking my hair while my mom was on the phone.

This is how my mom supported us: by sleeping around. I am not sure if there was any welfare money. I know for sure there were never any child welfare people checking on us. We were never in one place long enough for anyone to be able to track us down.

At age fifteen, I started to date. My mom would strut out to the car when my date dropped me off. She would be dressed all sexy, and she would lean into his car window and say, "Hey sexy boyfriend, when are you going to take me out?" I was so embarrassed. I did have a steady boyfriend for a while. During that time, I had a lot of anxiety. A lot had happened. This was after the drug gang broke into our house and gagged and tied up my brothers. They had guns, and I remember cracking my bedroom door open and seeing them down at the end of the hallway, so I ran and hid under my bed. I just remember it was a rough time, and it was all too much. Fortunately, my boyfriend's parents were kind enough to allow me to move in with them for a short while. That is until I was feeling better.

My mom even slept with her sister's husband. I found that

out years later. It helped to explain to me why we were not ever welcome at their house.

I never had any new clothes; all my clothes were hand-me-downs. One time, I took a pair of shorts from the used clothing bag and hand-sewed them to fit me. I added some fringe to dress them up. I decided to wear them to school the next day. My teacher asked me if I had made my shorts. I answered her that yes, I had. She then asked me to come up in front of the class. I thought I was going to die from embarrassment. I thought she was bringing me up to face my class so that they could make fun of my shorts. Much to my surprise, my teacher wanted to share how talented she thought I was and complimented me in front of the whole class. A compliment and kind words. Something I knew nothing about. Oh, Heavenly Father, thank You for my teacher and my feeling special on that day. I will remember that day and how I felt forever.

I never spoke about or told the truth about my home life at school. When I had a rare opportunity to go over to a friend's house, I was confused that their life was so different from mine. They weren't having red noodles with tomato soup for dinner. Their dad was not coming home drunk and beating his kids. My dad was a very mean drunk. Their dad was not fist-fighting with his alcoholic buddies in the backyard of their house. Their mom did not disappear for days, sometimes for months at a time.

When my dad was sober, which was not often, he was the nicest guy. I always wished and prayed for my dad to have more good days.

I have a memory of my dad having a girlfriend, and at some point, we were at the lake on vacation at his trailer. His girlfriend hated me. One time, she and my dad were in a terrible fight, and they were choking each other. They were trying to kill each other.

My dad would take his girlfriend to his family's get-togethers. It always caused problems. It always turned out bad.

My dad had three brothers and one sister. One brother committed suicide and had seven kids. Another brother had two sons who committed suicide. That brother was mean and nasty. He called me names. Seems like a whole lot of tragedy, ugliness, and meanness existed in this entire family.

My brothers were drug dealers. While we were all still living together, one day, a group of rival drug dealers forced their way into our house. My brothers were blindfolded, and they duct-taped their mouths shut. Fortunately, they didn't touch my brother, who had all the injuries from the car accident. I was able to hide in a tiny bedroom that looked like a closet. When the rival drug dealers were close to that door, he told them that it was just a closet and no one was in there. He said no one could even fit in there. They believed him. It was known to others that this one brother was not well enough to take part in any of the things that my other brothers did. So, they believed him. Those guys robbed my brothers of all their drugs and their drug money. It was terrifying, to say the least. Another time, our house was shot up by rival drug dealers. While I was in the kitchen one day, I heard gunshots. Our house was riddled with bullets by a rival gang.

I only went to school through the tenth grade. When I turned sixteen, my dad bought me a car for $150.00. I decided I was moving away. One day, I met my dad at the bar, and he was with his girlfriend. I told him I wanted to move away and I needed some money. His girlfriend shouted out, "Don't give her… any money." My dad dropped some cash on the floor for me. I stooped down, grabbed it up, and ran for the door with her chasing after me. Once out of there, I drove my car from Michigan to Florida. When I got there, I lied about my age, and I got a job as a bartender. I rented a run-down trailer. I had escaped from the nightmare I had been living. Sadly, I do not remember ever being told by my parents that they loved me. I also do not have any memories of any compliments. I wish that my dad could have said that he loved me the day that I ran off to Florida.

At twenty-five years old, I moved back to Michigan, where I met my first husband at a party. He was ten years older than me. We moved to the upper peninsula of Michigan. His name was Dave, and he was a nice guy. We had one daughter together. After seven or eight years, we ended up divorcing because even though he was a nice guy, he was an alcoholic and he used drugs.

Shortly after I divorced Dave, I met another man, and his name was Jake. Jake and I never married, but I did get pregnant. He was a bodybuilder, and he took a lot of steroids. He was really into himself, and he just did not want a baby. Jake wanted me to get an abortion. I refused, and I told him it was not an option. He then started claiming that there was no way this could be his child because he was sterile. He claimed he was sterile because of all the steroids he took. Our daughter was his baby. I honestly had not slept with anyone else.

After our daughter was born and she was just a few months old, I had her on the changing table. I asked Jake to watch her for a minute. When I returned, I was sickened to find that he had our daughters' legs spread apart and was looking and touching, not in a normal way. When I confronted him, he got angry. He held a loaded gun to my head and threatened me. What he did and what happened to our daughter was a big red flag for me, and we separated. After that shocking day, Jake was only allowed to have supervised visits with our daughter.

Unfortunately, my choice of men did not change. I seemed to be able to find the same kind of guy over and over again. They never started out that way. They seemed to be good in the beginning. I think my barometer was damaged. I continued to be attracted to the same type of guys over and over again. I desperately wanted to be loved. And everything that ever went wrong was always my fault. This is what I was always told growing up. It was always my fault; I had very low self-esteem.

I was on my own again with two daughters to care for. I worked as a waitress, I cleaned houses, and sometimes I worked at a party store to pay the bills. I also did some office work. I attended beauty school. I moved into my second-oldest brother's basement. My mom, at that time, was also living with him. My mom helped with caring for my daughters while I was working. We needed the money. Even though she did not have a good track record, I did what I had to do. I desperately needed help while I worked.

As I have already sadly shared, I was still dating dysfunctional, abusive, and alcoholic men. One of those men had a house. When he and I decided to break it off, I bought him out—so finally, I was a homeowner. I had worked hard, working several different jobs; I sincerely deserved this.

I was married to my second husband, Jack, for nineteen years. Jack and I dated in high school. I did not like him when we were in school, but I guess I saw something different about him years after. His family owned a successful bowling alley. They had a lake house, a hunting lodge, and a lot of property. They were a wealthy family.

While we were married, we did a lot together with his family. Eventually, Jack and I bought the bowling alley from his dad. Life seemed good. Jack treated me very well. We had money and a beautiful home, horses, and stables. He bought me many beautiful gifts. Jewelry was something he gifted me with often. I went from rags to riches. But sadly, the fairy tale life I was living eventually ended up not being what I thought it was, and after being married for nineteen years, I filed for divorce.

I divorced Jack because of finding out about all the women he was sleeping with. Then I had another heartbreaking surprise when I found out that he slept with the babysitter that he and his first wife used, and he had fathered a child with the babysitter. The child was a son, and by the time I found out about this boy, he was already ten years old. I also found out that he had been paying child support for this boy the entire time that we were married.

Jack and I had some mutual friends. But after the divorce, and after all the lies he talked about me to our friends and others, they chose sides, and it was not my side that they chose. It was no wonder because the lies that he told were hateful, awful, and untrue in his attempt to destroy me.

As I found out more and more, I learned that Jack slept with every girl who worked at the bowling alley. He also had ruined the business financially. He claimed none of it was his fault. He blamed me for all the financial losses. It was all my fault, he told everyone, and yet he was the one that ran everything. He brought paperwork home for me to take care of, but the cash he always kept. Who knows how much that was? I was just a billpayer for the business. I paid for the utilities and such. I did not even get a paycheck. Yet one of the women that he was sleeping with who worked at the bowling alley was making a big weekly salary.

We traveled all over the country together during what I thought were our good years together. He cheated on me then, too, and I found out he cheated on me before we even got married. He lied to me. He told me he was divorced and had a son. He moved in with me, and then his wife found out and filed for divorce. Jack's family and parents never liked me because they believed I broke up their marriage. I honestly thought he was divorced. I believed him. He love-bombed me. I fell for it all. I was a loyal and devoted wife to him because I loved him. I worked hard to please him.

After our divorce, I ended up in counseling for five years. I attended Lacasa, a center for abuse victims. I learned a lot. I heard other women's tragic stories who suffered abuse. I refer often to the book *Psychopath Free* by Jackson MacKenzie. They say knowledge is power. I needed to learn why I continued to choose over and over again the same toxic relationships. I also learned about sociopaths, too.

The driving force for sociopaths is to dominate others. They do this for the feeling of power and control.

Because sociopaths lack a conscience, they are willing to do anything to get what they want.

I learned a great deal about myself, and there was a lot I did not like. Not that I felt I was a bad person, but rather a victim who allowed the same record to keep playing. I had never heard of it before, but I suffered from Stockholm syndrome.

Many psychologists and medical professionals consider Stockholm syndrome a coping mechanism or a way to help victims handle the trauma of a terrifying situation. (Psychology Today)

Stockholm syndrome is a psychological response. It happens when abuse victims bond with their captors or abusers. This psychological connection develops over days, weeks, months, or even years of captivity or abuse. Some victims even develop positive feelings toward their captors.

Trauma bonding is also what I suffered, and it is similar to Stockholm syndrome, in which people held captive come to have feelings of trust or even affection for the very people who capture and hold them against their will. This type of survival strategy can also occur in any relationship. It can occur when a person is in a relationship with a narcissist.

Within a trauma bond, the narcissist's partner first feels loved and cared for. However, this begins to erode over time, and emotional, mental, and sometimes physical abuse takes over the relationship.

The codependent understands the change but not why it is occurring. They believe they just need to understand what they are doing wrong to bring back the loving part of the relationship.

If they do manage to break free, all the narcissists must do is go back to that courtship phase to win them back. Thus, the reason I repeatedly went back for more.

I also had EMDR therapy. That is an eye movement desensitization and reprocessing (EMDR) psychotherapy treatment. It was originally designed to alleviate the distress associated with traumatic memories. I was having a very hard time. I needed all the help I could get.

Jack's father died, and Jack was left with a big inheritance. We had been married for fifteen years at that time. His father was very well off. Plus, Jack was the golden boy. Many people speculated that Jack had a gambling problem. I believe all those special gifts that he gave to me were guilty gifts for all the cheating that he did. But something was happening to all the money. One bowling season, he stole all the prize money for the end-of-year bowlers' winnings and awards. He also sold a house on a land contract and then refinanced it.

It is heartbreaking to me that our daughter had a settlement from a serious car accident that she was in, and Jack borrowed that money with a promise to pay her back, and he never did.

During our marriage, I did start to save a little nest egg from grocery money, etc. A rainy day fund. Thank goodness I did because I would have been left with absolutely nothing. I saved for ten years, and it was enough to put a small down payment on a house. I received nothing when we divorced. No assets, no money. The children did not receive anything either.

When I filed for divorce, Jack became violent. This is also when he started a smear campaign against me and about me. He told lies about me to anyone who would listen. He made me out to be the bad guy.

During the divorce, he made this time hard on me. He got rid of the four-wheelers and the tractors, so I had a hard time caring for the horses. I had to get hay to the barn and water for the horses. I hauled it all by hand. I am a small person. It caused internal damage to my insides, and I also developed five hernias. All this resulted in major surgeries for me. During this stressful period, I slapped Jack one time, and he called the police and pressed charges. I spent the night in jail.

I know that he also had a $500,000 life insurance policy on me. I had one frightening experience where I thought he might have put something in my drink when we were out of town, and I became critically ill. There were also a few months during the divorce when I was very sick, and my brothers made mention to me to be careful; they thought he might be slowly poisoning me. It could be a coincidence, but I know now he felt desperate at this time and under a lot of pressure financially.

Keeping true to form after I divorced Jack, I hooked up with another psycho boyfriend, Biff. I was born on Easter Sunday. Easter is celebrated on a different day of the month each year, but it is always celebrated on a Sunday. Biff and I talked, and we decided it would be fun to take a trip to Washington, DC, to celebrate my birthday, and so we did. We arrived, checked into our hotel, and made our way around the city that first day. I was not expecting what happened next. It was 5:00 a.m. when the phone rang. This very early morning call was to tell me that Jack, my ex-husband, had committed suicide. He had taken a double-barrel shotgun, put it in his mouth, and shot himself. He was parked and sitting in his truck when he did it. I was in total disbelief.

Sickened, sad, hurt, shocked, so many emotions were washing over me. And he had killed himself on my birthday. Why was this? Why on my birthday?

His family would not allow me to attend the funeral. They blamed me. They said this was all my fault.

At that time, Jack had a girlfriend. The story I heard about this heartless girlfriend was that in the cab of Jack's truck was a ham he had bought for Easter dinner. I was told she took that blood-splattered ham out of the bed of his truck for her Easter dinner. I cannot begin to comprehend this.

I believe his suicide was planned because he left suicide notes for my two daughters and others. My daughters said they saw a letter on the table in his handwriting for me, too, but his girlfriend or someone else never gave it to me. I do not know what his last words were for me. I wish I knew. I was told that at the bowling alley on that day, he reminded everybody that it was my birthday. It seems like he wanted to make sure everybody knew this day was significant. I can't help but believe that this was his final present to me. Another way to hurt me. Every birthday, the first thing I remember is that he killed himself on my birthday.

Jack and I went to the same doctor during the nineteen years we were married. Sometime after Jack's death, I went in to see the doctor for a checkup. It was then that the doctor shared with me that he was happy to hear that I had been in Washington,

D.C., when Jack killed himself. Our doctor went on to say he felt this way because he was convinced that if I had not been out of town, he believed Jack would have committed a murder-suicide. That Jack would have killed me first and then killed himself.

I heard that the police thought perhaps Jack might have actually been murdered and that they even had a suspect, but the coroner had ruled it a suicide, so nothing ever came of it.

I did find a letter months later that Jack had written when I was going through some old things. In the letter, he said that I was a good wife and a good mother. It was comforting for me to read that.

I dated the psycho boyfriend, Biff, on and off for about three years. When we first met, he was so suave and cute. He preached the Bible, so I thought he was a good Christian man. After dating for three months, he moved in with me. Things were good for about six months. I was in love. He had me. We had fun together. We went to concerts and car shows, and we took vacations. Then, he started to disappear for a few days at a time without a good explanation. We broke up numerous times because of it. It is hard for me to admit, but I took him back twenty-seven times. He also had numerous affairs while we were together. I caught him, and my daughter caught him as well. He had a friend who died from an overdose that he was somehow connected to. Things were scary. I found out my Bible guy had been in prison for six years for theft and a stabbing incident. Another time, he filed a harassment charge against me, and I had to scrape together $1,000.00 to fight the charge in court.

I had to have surgery to repair the serious injuries I mentioned that I suffered while caring for our horses while I was going through my divorce from Jack. When I came home after having the surgery, Biff promised that he would help take care of me. That very first night, he did make me a sandwich. Then I asked him if he could please put the dog in the kennel. He snapped back and said, "You get off your ass and you do it. I worked all day."

Finally, one day, it was over for good. It was all too much. Then, I could not believe what I saw. From the mirror on the bathroom door, I could see Biff had my toothbrush, and he was swirling it around in the toilet as he was having a bowel movement. I hesitated and had second thoughts about even sharing this. What he did was so disgusting. But this is what evil looks like. This is what abuse and control look like. We can't sugarcoat the extent to which some of these unstable, mean, controlling, and evil people will go. We can't sugarcoat my emotional instability. I was brainwashed and broken, and I felt unworthy. And I am sorry to say this is only one disgusting example of the many things he did like that.

I feel like I had a neon advertising sign on my forehead that said, "Are you mean and bad? I'll take you. That's my specialty."

My dating with Biff has stopped, but he is still lurking and stalking me. It is four and a half years later. He has tried to poison my dog. He leaves things in my yard to let me know he has been there and that he is watching. I still find cigarette butts that are his brand behind the backyard of my house. He goes through my garbage. The police are unable to help unless he tries to break in or assault me.

At this time in my life am I healed? I know this book is about healing. I honestly probably will never be able to say that I am healed. But what I can share is that I am wiser. I have lived through so much. I have lived through so many hard lessons about life. I am in a better place. I am at peace. I know where to turn for help. But I am lonely. I sit in my recliner at night at home, alone, and I still long for someone to love me. I watch the door and wish for that special and loving someone to walk through my front door.

Boundaries are most important to me. I cannot trust getting too close to anyone. No more dating and no more marriages. Not for me. And, then again, I come right back to what I just said. I am lonely. I want to be loved.

I am not crazy. I'm reminded of the movie *Gaslight*, a 1944 American psychological thriller about a young woman whose husband slowly manipulates her into believing she is crazy. A narcissist.

In my life, did I pray? Yes, I did, but I struggled with trust and belief. There was a time in my life when prayer and God showed up big for me. I was diagnosed with a brain tumor. I had a prayer chain for my healing that stretched clear across the country. I went in for surgery, and when I came out of recovery, the doctor said they could not find the tumor. At first, they thought they had the wrong location of where the tumor was. They scheduled another MRI. Again, those results showed no sign of a tumor. Prayers were answered. I have had sixteen different surgeries, and God has brought me through them all.

I do feel that I deserve a better life. For most of my life, I have felt less about myself, unworthy, not good enough. I know that I did my very best to be a good wife and mother. I know how to love deeply.

I take time to enjoy the beauty of God's creations all around me. The birds, the ocean, the blue skies, and more. And my two dogs bring me so much happiness and love. After all the pain in my life, I still have love and compassion. I feel good about helping others and those in need. The elderly, veterans, and others. I know what it feels like to be desperate and in need of help. While I am still able to, with the time that I have left, I want to feel good about life and what I can give back to those in need. I want my life to count for something.

I share this special wisdom from my heart with others:

Escape if you are in a bad situation. Learn from my mistakes and misfortunes. You deserve better. Reach out; there is help for you. Some people care.

Read your Bible and get to know God.

Heal your life!

Chapter Six:

The National Orphans Home Was an Institution with High Ideals

CAROL METCALF'S INTERVIEW AND STORY.

My chapter and personal story are different from most of the other chapters in this book. However, my story is an important addition because it sheds light on broken systems. Systems that need *healing* because they are broken and are sometimes more harmful than good. Specifically, broken systems and policies that exist within the foster care system and orphanages that are providing for and caring for children. I want you to know it could be better.

My story begins with this: "If it's not broken, don't try to fix it."

There was an orphanage in existence for several years that housed thousands of children who shared many good memories, special bonds, and feelings of gratefulness.

My mom grew up in an orphanage, and to many people's surprise, she smiled whenever she talked about it. There was something different that set this orphanage apart from the others. The kids that lived there were not called orphans; they were called

Home Kids. Thousands of other kids grew up in this orphanage and had happy memories that they proudly shared as well.

The sign at the entrance read:

National Orphans Home

The Institution of High Ideals

The Largest Institution of its Kind in the United States

Located in Tiffin, Ohio

Most often, when we think of orphanages, the picture we get in our mind and the stories that we hear are about children who are sad, lonely, dirty, unloved, and even some who were abused. Their reasons for ending up in an orphanage are, in most cases, from tragic situations.

This home that set the bar at the very top was The Junior Order of United American Mechanics National Orphans Home, Jr. O.U.A.M. It began and opened in 1850. It had a name change in 1896 and then closed its doors in 1944.

The need for this home and the organization of the American Mechanics order came about during a time in our history when our country was suffering through government and economic policies that deeply affected the quality of life for many American citizens.

Between 1820 and 1860, millions of immigrants flocked to American cities. The peak period was between 1847 and 1857.

During those ten years, 3.3 million immigrants entered the United States. 1.3 million were from Ireland, and 1.1 million were from the German states. There was much hatred and resentment among American citizens against the immigrants because they were taking their jobs. American citizens also saw the government rewarding immigrants and doling out numerous benefits for them based solely on nationality rather than merit. Along with this, the actions that the Roman Catholic Church started enforcing also intensified anti-foreign sentiment.

The American Mechanics' purpose was to form a secret society for the protection of their jobs. The first meeting of the order was held on July 8, 1845.

The name of the order was later changed to the Association of the Order of United American Mechanics.

There were six objectives for the order:

1. To assist each other in obtaining employment.

2. To assist each other in business by patronizing each other in preference to foreigners.

3. To assist the unfortunate in obtaining employment suitable to their afflictions.

4. To establish a cemetery for deceased members of society.

5. To establish a funeral fund.

6. To establish a fund for the relief of widows and orphans

of deceased members.

The Junior Order billed itself as patriotic and inspired by the ideals of virtue, liberty, and patriotism.

It was object number six, to establish a fund for the relief of widows and orphans of deceased members, that grew the start of needing a home for "the Home Kids." Mothers were not able to clothe and feed their children when their husband and father of their children suddenly lost their lives. This happened often because of their working conditions in the mines. Upon a father's death, his income ceased. It was a hopeless situation for many families.

Tiffin, Ohio, was chosen for the location of the national orphanage for the Junior Order. It was patterned after the Cottage Plan, which, at the time, had worked well in other areas of the country. The Jr. Home became a self-sufficient fifty-building residential complex on 850 acres.

Many of the mothers felt guilty sending their children to the home, even though they knew they were without any other good options for taking care of them. It was harder on the mothers than it was on the children. Many of the kids arriving at the home had no shoes, they had been living without any running water, they were tired, and they were hungry.

The order saw and felt that it had a responsibility to be *father-like* in the absence of the biological father of the Home Kids. The cottages very much mimicked home life living. Having individual cottages allowed for smaller family groups to stay together as opposed to a big institutional-type building. The orphanage also had a hospital. The only hospital in Tiffin.

My grandmother Mary's life as she knew it, and the lives of their five children, drastically changed when her husband John died at the age of thirty-two from swine flu and pneumonia. My mother, Juanita, was one of those five children. She was born on February 9, 1914, even though she never had a birth certificate, which sometimes occurred years ago. They were a family of three girls and two boys, all under the age of nine when he died. Her father, John M. Johnson, was born September 30, 1888, in Virginia. He married my grandmother, Mary Love, on December 5, 1910. They lived in New Market, Tennessee, and then moved to Mascot, Tennessee, where my grandfather took a job working in a zinc mining company. My grandfather was a hoister for the zinc mining company called Holston Zinc Mine in Mascot, Tennessee. A hoister hoisted workers and equipment in and out of the mine. Because of the harsh working conditions, he developed and suffered from black lung disease and TB, when suddenly he came down with swine flu and pneumonia. His death left his wife of nine years a young widow and mother with five children and no income or means for her to support their family. My grandmother's family was not able to take in six people. At the time my grandfather died, my mother was just four years old. Sadly, she barely knew her father.

There was no Social Security, WIC programs, welfare…

nothing to help my grandmother. Social Security was not put into place until several years later, in 1935. Fortunately, six months before John died, he had joined the Mechanics Union. That decision proved to be a major blessing, especially because of the orphanage benefit. Such an important benefit for the miners and their families because of the dangerous exposure they had to work each day. For an initiation fee of five dollars, these five children could be sent to the National Orphans Home in Tiffin. Here, they would be housed, clothed, fed, schooled, and taught a trade until they were age eighteen. My grandmother would have to relinquish all legal rights to her children and then make their way by train to Tiffin, Ohio. And so she did. My mother, just four years old and on a train headed to the orphanage. The five children were aged six months and two, four, six, and eight years. In April 1919, they arrived in Tiffin, where Grandmother Mary surrendered four of her five children. The baby was too young for the home and had to be left with Mary. This was a problem for her because she could not get a job. After all, she had no one to watch over the baby. So, Mary and the baby went to Cincinnati to live with Mary's mother until the baby was old enough to be accepted by the home. At one point, Mary was so distraught she sent a letter to the Junior Order Home asking, begging them to please take her baby because she could not get a job and take care of herself and her baby.

The Home was absolutely a godsend. Located on an eight-hundred-and-fifty-acre plot in Tiffin, Ohio, the home was self-contained. Cottages, as they were called (more like English two-story houses), were built by each state's Junior Order Home members. A dining hall that held eight hundred was built, and the home's cows provided milk for more than a thousand children. Pigs, steers, and vegetables were grown on the farm to feed the children. The canning department prepared forty-five thousand quarts of vegetables a year for the children's meals. But perhaps the best part of the Home was the school. All children, even mentally challenged children, went to school for half a day. The other half was spent learning a trade. More than twenty-five different trades were taught, including anything from cabinet making to greenhouse work to dressmaking to printing. My mother chose printing. Because the Home recognized her intelligence, she was moved from the seventh grade to the ninth grade. As her printing skills increased, so did the demand for printed materials. The students from the printing class were responsible for printing everything that was left and circulated out of the Junior Order Home newspaper that had a subscription of thirty thousand per month. The Home had just about everything a child would want: a swimming pool, football team, musical instruments, plays, etc.

The five siblings could see each other every day, even though they lived in different cottages over the years. They could even visit their mother occasionally on weekends or in the summer.

In 1902, Charles Henry "Dad" Kern was hired as superintendent. The meeting notes from this point on, and for each year thereafter while he was in charge, showed marked improvement. This continued year after year until the doors closed. He encouraged excellence, virtue, respect, and duty in all the children. Under his leadership, the children developed a strong sense of honor, pride, loyalty, and responsibility.

My mother was fortunate to be under his guidance, and so were her siblings. The school had over fifty vocational courses, church, sports teams, farming, recreation, and more. The children formed deep, lasting bonds that expanded well past their time together while living at home. This model worked well. It is most unfortunate that it was phased out.

The orphanage felt the highest service they needed to provide was to discover the potential and the proper correlation of each student to help them find the special work in life that suited them best.

Students from ten years of age and upward were taught how to make furniture, which included woven baskets, davenports, chairs, tables, lamps, and more. My mother's souvenir book, which she was given upon graduation, shared a list of the valuable vocations that were available to the children.

The list is:

- Household economy
- Greenhouse work
- Woodworking
- Printing
- Cabinet making
- Newspaper

- Lathe work
- Practical nursing
- Canning
- Auto repair
- Carpentry
- Bakery
- Art fiber
- Shoe repair
- Plumbing
- Moving picture operating
- Painting
- Chef (kitchen)
- Laundry
- Store clerking
- Stationery
- Dressmaking
- Farming
- Instrumental music
- Truck farming.

On Saturday and Sunday, the older children at the orphanage were allowed to go into town to see a movie or enjoy the park. Thousands of children lived, laughed, thrived, and went on to live good lives. The testament of proof is still shared today as the generations that followed the Home Kids still gather and reunite to celebrate this special bond.

My grandmother remarried three years after my grandfather died, and she had two more children. The year was 1922, and she was thirty-two years old. Her new husband unfortunately turned into an alcoholic. My mother shared with me that it was hurtful that my grandmother did not try to get her children from her first marriage back home to live with her. She left all five of them in the orphanage. "Why could she take care of those two kids and not take us back?" The reality was there were just too many of them.

My mom was very smart and was able to graduate at age seventeen in 1931. She graduated with a trade school education titled Commercial Class of Study. The class motto was "Not Evening But Dawn." She had to leave the orphanage at age eighteen, which was the maximum age for all children. My mother had to build a new life because she was no longer a Home kid. She moved in with her older sister, who was living in Tiffin. She stayed working at the print shop at the orphanage until 1939. The printing department was responsible for everything the Home sent out, including the newspaper called *The Junior American*. However, things were changing for Mom. All her siblings were married. She was feeling left out. So, when World War II broke out, she and a friend went to North Carolina to work in a factory for the war effort. She was only there for less than a year and came home alone and very homesick. She had never been away from her brothers and sisters. It was just too much.

As good as life as my mother had at the Home, she was always missing something. While the home treated her very well, fed her, schooled her, and housed her, she lacked a mother's love. No one had ever told her how smart she was, how organized, or how pretty she was. No one had told her what a fun-loving, kind person she was. Her self-esteem was at a low point. By now, she was looking for someone to love and unfortunately found the wrong person. In 1948, she married a man who had a violent temper and beat her. She escaped him and went to her sister's house for comfort. Her brother-in-law said she was never to go back to him, and said that Mom could live with them. Mom divorced him after less than six months of marriage. Wanting to escape him and Tiffin, she moved forty miles away to her sister's and brother-in-law's, who said they would take her in. She got a good job as an executive secretary and made good money. Life in the small-town village was good, and two years later, she went on a blind date and met my dad. Six months later, they were married. Two years later, they got an unexpected surprise. My mom found out at the age of thirty-eight that she was pregnant with me. My dad was forty-eight. Surprise-surprise!

I never met my grandmother. Since my mother knew what it felt like to grow up without a mother and as an orphan, she tried extra hard to be the best possible mother she could be for me. She always gave me wonderful guidance and advice. My mom did with me all the things that she never experienced. She read to me incessantly. She played games with me. She taught me how to add and subtract while playing Crazy Eights. She was my biggest fan, friend, and confidant. Many of my friends would comment and say they wished their mom was more like my mom.

She cautioned me to watch out for the bad apples, which were the guys she said would try to take advantage of me. She told me about a guy named Gray Lake who took her out on a boat. He thought that he could have his way with her because he had her out in the middle of the lake. She told me to never allow myself to be put in that kind of situation. She always had good advice for me.

When I was in college, I got a proofreading job, and my mother loved to help; she was extremely good at it. She loved puzzles, Scrabble, and sports. Her brother Rob had played football for the team at the orphanage. Her sister Alvena could sing beautifully, and she was good at gymnastics. My mother was also good at many things, and most of all, I always admired her for her patience. She was so smart, but what she lacked was self-confidence.

It has been talked about, all through the years, that moving away from the mining town in Tennessee and to the orphanage allowed for so many more opportunities that my grandmother's children would not have otherwise had.

My mother was sixty-six when she died from a heart attack. I was devastated to lose my best friend and my amazing mother. She was always there for me, coached, guided, and supported me every step, and because of it, I furthered my education, which included getting my master's degree.

My mother's siblings also have successful children who then, too, had successful children who achieved many great accomplishments in their lives. Some of those successes include working for major corporations like being the Global Human Resource Manager for the Air Jordan division of Nike. What does all this say about the possibilities we have in life? You can grow up without living with a father and a mother and suffer tragedies, but don't ever let that stop you from believing for more and that you deserve more. Thousands of kids who were poor little orphans living at the National Orphans Home in Tiffin, Ohio, are proof of that.

If it's not broken, then please don't try to fix it. This orphanage model worked very well. The children thrived, and then along came a new regime with a new system and closed the orphanage. My hope by telling this story is that it raises awareness regarding the long-term success that lives on in the families. The families of the orphan children who grew up in the United American Mechanics National Orphans Home. They were not orphans; they were proud Home Kids.

I dedicate this story to my mother, Juanita. My mother worked for many years in the print shop. She was very passionate about sharing stories with others. I know in my heart she would be extremely happy to know by telling this story we are shedding light on a place and a time when they got it right. And because of it, it made a positive difference in the lives of thousands of children.

CHAPTER SEVEN:

I THOUGHT IF I COULD JUST SURVIVE UNTIL I TURNED EIGHTEEN, MY LIFE AFTER THAT WOULD BE COMPLETELY DIFFERENT

MARIA'S INTERVIEW AND STORY.

Sometimes, we look at other people who seem to be doing well and wonder how they got so lucky in life. What is their magic formula? Everything about them seems almost perfect. The way they look, the way they laugh, the way they smile. The clothes they wear, the way they walk and talk, all so seemingly confident in themselves. Those fortunate people make life look so easy, happy, and carefree.

Our childhood is our foundation. Our building blocks. Much like the foundation of a house. It can be a strong foundation or a weak foundation. A good foundation or a bad foundation. And built on top of that foundation are the walls of a child's life and the family or people they are living with.

So, what life looks like through the eyes of that small child growing up is whatever they are living and what is going on between those walls. This home could be with or without parents.

It could be stepparents, grandparents, or even a foster home. It could be a happy home or an unhappy home. It could be an abusive home with beatings and punishments so bad that it would be hard to survive. Tragically, many children are trapped between evil walls, and some don't make it out alive. And if they do make it out, some of them turn into offenders themselves, drug addicts, alcoholics, and other tragic existences.

My childhood growing up was an absolute living nightmare. Every day, I lived in fear, not knowing what or how bad the abuse was going to be that day. The only thing I knew for sure was there would be abuse. Sexual, physical, and verbal abuse. You can be sure of that. I knew I was not even safe when I went to bed at night. You always slept lightly, never soundly, because you had to listen closely for the footsteps. When you heard even the slightest creak in the floor, you knew soon the door would fling open, and the nightmare would begin. What would happen to you tonight?

My siblings and I suffered physical, sexual, and verbal abuse. As a very small girl, I lived for a few years in foster care, and I thought that my life was really hard then. But in comparison, my life growing up with my mother's second husband and my stepfather was nothing short of a living hell. It was a living hell for myself, my siblings, and my mother. I can't even begin to paint or give a good descriptive picture of myself to be able to help you truly know how bad my bruises, belt lashes, and rubber hose marks were. Or my bloody nose and mouth, swollen black eyes, and cigarette burn marks. The blows to my ear that left me deaf for weeks. I also can't find the words to help describe the sheer terror, the physical pain, the broken heart, and the feelings of worthlessness, being stupid and unloved. What I can't believe the most is how I even survived it, and I can tell my story. I can't believe my siblings and my mother lived through it, either. These are just words on a piece of paper. But if I can help to describe the awful truth about the nightmare that we lived in, you need to know that there were many days we felt we would have rather died.

But for all of us, even though we survived and made it out, you never forget, and the nightmares never really stop. It gets easier, but the trauma is always lingering. Hear a harsh word, see a child being hit, and it all comes rushing back in. Darkness and fear set in.

As a young child growing up, when I was around and saw some of the happy children at school, it caught my attention. I started to be aware that life for those children seemed to look a whole lot different from mine. I think I started studying them. I started to pay close attention to how they talked, dressed, and how smart they were. I liked what I saw, and I wanted to be more like them. I wanted the fairytale life they had. I started dreaming about it. I started believing I could have it. Thinking about this was so much better for me to focus on instead of hopelessness and helplessness. Yes, there was still abuse and pain in my life every day, but having this to hope for helped. *Maybe I can't have that better life right at this time*, I thought, *but someday when I turn eighteen, I can leave home.*

We had strict rules at our house. You had better keep quiet about what was going on in our house. You talked to no one about what went on in our house, and you were never allowed to bring friends home. You covered up and hid any marks and signs of physical abuse, and if anyone suspected something, you had better lie about what happened. Our telling our teachers that we had accidentally tripped and fallen down the stairs was used often. That, along with a lot of other made-up accidents that we supposedly had. You were also not allowed to feel bad or sorry for yourself. And if you did, you would get a worse beating than the one you just had. And you should always feel shame because you were worthless, stupid, and no good for anything. A therapist could write a whole book just about us and our devastatingly dysfunctional family life.

I watched my mother, too. Through all that she suffered, the life-threatening beatings and verbal abuse that she took from my stepfather, she still stayed strong and showered her love over all of us. She stood up for us and paid the price for it every single time. My stepfather threatened her that if she ever tried to leave, she would lose her children. She would never see us again. So, she stayed with us and protected us the best that she could. At times, he beat her so badly I would think to myself, *This is it. He has killed her for sure this time.*

Her strong courage and love are the qualities I wanted for

myself. I admired my mother. She was a rock, and she loved me. She loved us all. I listened and watched, and I learned from her. And so, I continue to try and live my life with that same love and passion. My mother also had a strong faith in God. That strong faith kept her alive. Her most precious saying was, "I am not worried. God will provide." She helped me to have that same strong faith in God, to believe that I deserved better and that I could have better. I was saved and baptized at age seventeen. My faith is still strong today, and He helps me through the storms in life.

Because I deeply knew what it felt like to suffer abuse, I knew that when I was able to finally escape the unbearable house I was living in, my life would be different. I thought a lot about this. If I say I thought about this a lot, I mean it was the most important vision in my mind from the time I woke up until I went to bed. I think it helped me to survive. It gave me strength and hope. Like the Bible verse that says, "This too shall pass."

I thought if I could just live through this until I turned eighteen, my life after that would be completely different. And it was, and it is.

Once I escaped it, I went down the path I promised God that I would. I had promised Him many times that if I could survive all this, when I was safe and away from all this, I would be compassionate and loving for others. I developed a strong sense of wanting to help others. To rescue them, to help take care of others. I knew desperation; I knew what it felt like to have no place to turn. I also knew pain. The kind of pain from beatings that leaves scars and reminders of how bad your life was. I could have turned out to be an abuser. So many victims follow the same path and become abusers themselves.

I know others who have had a hard life and who went down the same dark path they grew up in. Being hateful and ugly to others.

Your life can be better. You must push yourself. The abuse does not get erased just because it's not still happening; the abuse does not get erased or disappear. I even worried I would be a bad parent because I had lived through so much ugliness. I also suffered shame, so helping others helped me to feel good about myself. No one ever expected that my siblings or I would ever amount to anything. We were known as *throw-away children.*

"We are the choices we make." I recall this quote often made by someone years ago.

I also quote Bible verses to help me.

"Those who hope in the Lord will renew their strength, they will soar on wings like eagles, and they'll run and not grow weary" (Isaiah 40:31, NIV).

When I am torn apart by the storms in life, my prayers and faith in God calm me, comfort me, and remind me He is near. I am protected.

I love spending time at the beach. The ocean breeze, the

waves, it all brings a calmness to the inside turmoil that wants to resurface. The panic that starts to churn inside me. The triggers, the motion picture replays. No matter how many years have gone by, the flash in your brain hits, and it consumes your thoughts. I start with heavy breathing, and then I feel sick to my stomach. It is time for a cleanse. I look forward to the time that I can get to the beach. Until then, I spend time in the sunshine, taking long, deep breaths and long, soulful walks.

I would want others to find their place. That place that brings you peace, balance, and serenity. It could be the beach, high up on a hill, or a walk in the park. Because without that sense of wellness, security, and healing you struggle to maintain. You struggle to want to go on. Life is worth living. Start a new canvas and paint for yourself a much better picture of your life.

Chapter Eight:

I Prayed—Please, Dear God, Give Me A Sign. And So He Did, on the Day that My Mother Died

SANDY'S INTERVIEW AND STORY.

My mother had once asked me what I missed most about leaving my home in California. Most people might say the weather, the mountains, or the oceans, but for me, being an outdoors gal and a true nature lover, it was the giant red-tail hawks. My mother had cancer, and on the day that she died, I not only felt a heartbreaking stab to my heart because my mother was gone, but at the same time, I was at a place in my life where I so desperately needed to know that there truly was a God and that He cared about me. My marriage was failing, I was unhappy, and now my mother had lost her fight with cancer. As I cried out to God, with tears flooding my eyes and streaming down my face, suddenly, out of nowhere, this giant red hawk appeared and flew across my windshield as I was driving. I knew at that very moment that this was the sign from God that I had been praying for. There could not have been a better or bigger sign from God and an answer to my prayers at a time when I so desperately needed it. From that day forward, the courage and strength that I needed to endure and get through some very tough times came from my faith in God and remembering that day.

Going through my divorce from my high school sweetheart was a very hard road for me to go down. I took my wedding vows very seriously, and I felt like I had failed. But I took pride in our two sons that we were blessed with. In my heart, I knew getting a divorce was the best for both of us. Our marriage was ending because of indifference. I wrote a poem about indifference. I was still very much in love with him, but I did not feel loved. He had shut me out as though I was not there anymore. He stayed away from home as much as possible, and when he was home, he was mostly quiet and kept to himself. I wanted to go our separate ways on good terms because I truly loved him. I was determined to be kind and not hurtful, no matter what.

I did not date after the divorce until more than a year had gone by. I was in a good place in my life. I was enjoying spending time doing some of the things I had always hoped and wanted to do. I still had a lot of things on the back burner. So, I was not looking for someone to date. Things for me were good. I was good.

I love to line dance, and I knew that I didn't need a partner for that. So, my nights going out were with my girlfriends, and we would go line dancing. One night, a polite man named Mark approached me and asked, "Are you Sandy? Someone told me that I should come over and ask you to dance." I responded to him by saying yes, that I was Sandy, but I declined his invitation to dance by saying to him, "No, thank you." He didn't seem insulted or upset, and instead, he decided to invite himself to sit down and talk. I was sipping a Coke, and he had a beer. We talked for a long while. He seemed nice, and so when he asked me a second time if I would like to dance, I said, "Yes, I would."

Before I go on, I want to bring up the importance of recognizing red flags! Something that I am still working on.

I am working hard to become a better me. I know I have a lot of wonderful qualities, and I try to be a good person. But where I think I come up short is my being foolish, naïve, or whatever you would call it, but it is my weakness for not recognizing the red flags in life. The signs that say, "Look out, danger ahead! Stop now because this won't turn out well for you." All the warning signs are there, yet my kindness, care, and consideration of others camouflage over the other person's bad intentions. It is like my brain turns off all my warning signals. I ask myself, "What is wrong with me? Where did my childhood and life programming get so badly off track that I continue to get this wrong?" Because of it, I have suffered abuse, heartbreak, and even many times, I have been in fear for my very life.

One day, Mark asked me if I would like to see "Mark's World." We had been casually seeing each other at the same place where we had first met and line danced. I would like to say—this was my first red flag. He wanted me to ride with him in his truck to his house. I was not comfortable with that so I suggested that I would just follow him to his house in my car.

I felt safer having my own car. We drove for quite a distance down a long country road. Because I was a bit nervous about the situation I had just put myself in, I decided to give his home address to three of my girlfriends. As I was driving to his home, I reached out to each of them. As we turned off the road to enter his driveway, it felt like I was driving through the enchanted forest. Both sides of the driveway had long rows of tall evergreens. It was dark and secluded, and the driveway stretched a long way back from the road to the house. My heart was pounding, and I was a bit frightened and shaky, wondering if I had made a mistake. Once inside, to my relief, Mark was the perfect gentleman while showing me around the house. As time went on, it became a thing for us to spend time at his house. It was truly beautiful there. We would sit outside on the back patio and watch the deer eating a short distance from us. He made me feel special. He loved everything I said and did, and we both seemed very happy. I loved the outdoors and nature, and it all seemed so perfect.

One day, Mark said, out of the blue, "Let's go to the jewelry store and buy you a ring." My being surprised by this is an understatement. We drove to the jewelry store that was in a small shopping center, and I was a bit confused about what this ring that I was about to pick out was supposed to be for. He had not asked me to marry him. He had not proposed. So, I looked for something simple but nice and then asked him, "Are you going to ask me to marry you?" He said, "I already have in so many ways." He seemed a bit irritated because I was even asking this. He went on. He said he also had decided that he did not want us to tell my sons or his children. At this point, neither of us had even met each other's children. He went on to say that he did not want to tell them about anything until after we were married. I didn't feel good about that and told him that I was not comfortable with it. I told him I thought that my boys' feelings would be hurt. He firmly explained that this is how it is going to be. So, from that, I understood that it was either his way or not at all. He then went on and shared that we would be married in a church. His mother, her husband, and my dad could attend, and nobody else. Then, after the ceremony, all of us would go out to dinner. I was also told I was not allowed to bring any of my furniture and personal belongings into his house after we were married. I was only allowed to bring my clothes. He told me the reason was because he did not want my memories from my past in his house. This was our new beginning, starting fresh. He explained that he wanted to buy us all new things to start our newly married lives together. Red flag: He never bought one new thing during the entire time that we were married and together in that house. We were married and lived together in that house for seven years. It still breaks my heart because I gave up some personal belongings that I dearly loved.

The very day that we were married, he announced that he wanted me to quit my job. I had a good job that I liked, and it paid me well. I thought this might be a red flag, but then I dismissed it, thinking it was because he loved me so much and wanted to take care of me and make my life easier.

Soon, his drinking became more and more, and soon, I was not allowed out of the house by myself. Not even to the library or the store. None of my friends were allowed over. I belonged to him.

I had always had a dog, and I missed having one. He had told me a story early on that, at one point in his life, he had raised German shepherds. I decided that I would start the conversation with him about wanting a dog, and since he had raised them, he would probably want a German shepherd, too. He listened and then said, "Yes, but there are stipulations." His stipulations would make it impossible to get a German shepherd, and he knew it. He put the limit on spending at $500.00, and it could only be purebred. Certain cities and towns he would not approve of getting a dog from, and the list went on and on. He made it impossible, and I grew weary and sad as he completely squashed all my hopes. Until one day, I said that I just didn't care anymore and that I had decided that I did not want a dog anymore. I was over it. Well, that sent him into a wild rage. Suddenly, he began throwing chairs at me, then dishes, all the while yelling that I needed to follow his rules. He had given me specific details from the very beginning about what would be required to get a dog. I was terrified by all this. It was crazy.

After this episode, I let a little time go by, and then I decided to ask his mom for help. With her help, suddenly the price was raised to $1000.00, and then up to $1500.00, but then he still found another reason. Eventually, by some miracle, I finally got my precious German shepherd dog. But now my poor dog had lots of rules to abide by, too. The dog was only allowed in the kitchen, dining room, and basement. Now, I am worried about the well-being of the dog and myself. It was getting increasingly scary to live with him. I was always on eggshells, and he had so many rules. One day, while I was outside with the dog, he approached me and asked me why the dog was wet. I explained that the dog had been out by the swamp and had gotten wet there. Before I knew what was even happening, he grabbed the dog and dragged her along the ground with her squealing, all the way back to the swamp. He started throwing tree limb after tree limb into the swamp, all the while screaming at me as if I was completely stupid. Saying, "Didn't you know the swamp was dangerous with all the dead trees? A tree branch could puncture her and kill her." The swamp was nowhere for a dog. So, another rule has just been made by him, and I had better never forget it. The dog was not allowed anywhere near the swamp ever again.

There was even a rule for mopping floors. You had to mop in circles. No back-and-forth mopping was allowed, and if he showed you how to do something and you didn't follow his rules and instructions, you knew you would have to pay the price, and you would be punished for it.

One morning, I was preparing his breakfast, and I noticed that one of his egg yolks had broken when I put it on the plate. I said to him softly and sweetly, "I'm sorry, honey, but I just noticed that one of your egg yolks is broken, and I will fix you a new one." Without hesitation, he grabbed the plate and whipped it at me. It flew into the sink and broke. I was shocked, shaking, and terrified. My immediate thought was to open the door to the garage to escape. I went for it. I climbed inside my car, locked the doors, and stayed in there. On more than one occasion, when he went into one of his rages, I would sleep in my car all night. I remember thinking, and I would ask myself, while locked in my car in the dark, "Why was I allowing him to treat me this way?"

When I finally felt it might be safe to go back in the house he would be waiting, and he would say to me, "Are you ready to talk about this?" Then, he would add that I needed to understand that he loved me and that I was important to him. And as soon as he said those words, his rage started all over again. I promise you this sure didn't feel like love.

I started noticing the signs of when to expect the next rage. His foot might start to twitch, or he had other nervous motions. At this time, he was now drinking twelve beers every night. I had to keep them rotated by putting some in the freezer to keep them colder but being careful not to let them freeze. When he needed his next beer, he would hold his empty bottle up in the air, wave it back and forth, and say, "Mabel, another Black Label." Being the dutiful little wife that I was, I would walk over to take his empty bottle and promptly return with another beer for him that was temperature-perfect. He had complete control.

One day, I felt the strong need to say it, because it just flew out of my mouth: "I think I see why you think the way you do."

He instantly flared up and lunged at me, grabbing me by the hood of my sweatshirt, and then shoved me to the floor and then started kicking me. I tried to roll myself up into a ball to protect myself the best that I could, and all the while, he was still kicking me. I was gasping for air and praying to dear God to let this be over. *Please, make him stop.* Suddenly, he got scared because he knew he had lost complete control of himself. He started to panic. He thought I would try to get to my car and leave. That is if I could get my keys. I slowly got up, and so he ran to grab my keys before I could. I managed to get to the garage, and there I locked myself in the car. He stood outside the door and used the keys to unlock the door, and I would have to react as fast as possible to push the lock back down before he could grab me. This went on for what seemed like forever. He would dangle the keys at the window, taunting me, saying, "You want these?" Finally, he left the keys on the ground outside the car door. But then I was too afraid to unlock the door to grab them off the floor. I feared that maybe I wouldn't be able to do it fast enough, and he would grab me. I was terrified. I had to wait him out. Finally, after a long time, I went for it. I was able to grab the keys and lock myself in. I immediately started the car, and I drove myself to the police station. I sat outside the station for a long while, and then my phone started ringing. I hadn't even realized that my phone was in the car. That was a blessing. It was his mother calling, and she was begging me to go back home. She did ask if I was okay, so he must have told her something. She then said she was afraid that her son Mark was going to try and kill himself. This episode must have scared him because, from that day forward, when we slept in bed together, he would drape an arm over me and a leg over my hip to make sure that I was locked down and unable to get away. It was hard to sleep and even harder for me to breathe.

Because of this, he suddenly decided to give me a little bit of leeway. I was now allowed to go out to see a movie once in a while, but I had rules that I needed to follow. I had to report to him, and he had to know my whereabouts at all times. One day, I forgot to call, and when I returned home, I was punished for it.

I was not allowed to lock the bathroom door, so I would open a drawer of the vanity. That prevented the door from opening all the way to keep him from coming in. He seemed satisfied if he could jiggle the door handle, and he knew the door was not locked. This was my safe space. I would sit in the tub and write poetry. I often asked God, while alone and sitting in there, why was this happening to me—this had been my life now for seven years. During that time, I wrote seven books of poetry that I safely hid in the bathroom.

My dad suffered a stroke, and I got the call about him when I was out of the house and in the car driving somewhere that day. I immediately called Mark and told him what had happened to my dad and said to him that I was headed straight to the hospital to be with my dad. He yelled on the phone and said that I was not allowed to go. "Absolutely not," he said. I had better come home. He reminded me that, per the Bible, I belonged to him and not my dad. My place was with my husband, not my dad. I asked him if this was a threat. I think it was!

In the days that followed, I wanted to visit my dad as often as possible. I was going no matter what. Mark told me that if something went wrong with the car going back and forth, not to bother calling him. He would not help me. One day, the car was acting up, so I had it checked, and it was because the fan belts were all sliced up. The next day, I had a flat tire. The following day, another issue. It terrified me to think he would gamble with my life by messing with the car. He truly didn't care about me. This was no coincidence. I was taking a risk, but I didn't care.

There was another shocking event when I stopped to get gas. My credit card would not work, and I had no money. I immediately called the credit card company to ask why, and they connected me to the fraud department.

I was stunned. "Really?" I said, "The fraud department?" and then I asked why. They told me the owner of the card said that I needed his permission to use the card. I begged to differ, but they informed me I was wrong; I was not an account holder. So next, I called my sister, and she brought me $100.00 so that I could pay for gas and to be able to have some cash.

Mark and I decided we would start seeing a minister. At one of our sessions, Mark stormed out, and the minister looked at me and said, "I am afraid for you." On the way home, Mark almost hit three cars because of his raging anger. He skidded the car into the driveway. He dropped me off, and then he drove off. He came back at about 8:00 p.m. that night. He showered, came out naked, and sat on the floor by the fireplace. He told me that he wanted me out of his life. Shocked and scared, I walked to the bedroom and grabbed a bag that I had already half-packed with a few things in it. I came back out to where he was sitting by the fireplace. He spoke and said, "Get your dog and get out." I thought for a second about getting my dog, but it would put me too close for him to be able to grab me. I feared he would grab me and then beat me, and I feared I might not make it out this time. So, I went straight to the garage, I got in my car, and I drove off.

The next day, I went to the bank because I had left without any money. I wasn't prepared for what I found out. I was told that all our accounts had been closed and all of the money had been withdrawn. The manager kindly took me into her office and told me that Mark had been in and closed out all the accounts. My social security was being deposited into those accounts. I had to sort this out. I was blindsided. I called and tried to talk to him, and I met with him and told him his actions did not say he loved me.

In the days that followed, he kept calling me and telling me he loved me. I never answered the phone, but I did listen to the messages that he left. I filed for divorce; I wanted this craziness to be over. It wouldn't be easy. I needed to rebuild my credit and start a new life. For seven years, I had lived in this nightmare.

Over our seven years of marriage, I was told to get out a total of seven times. Each of those times I left, I had suffered another raging and abusive attack by him. Most people are shocked that I kept going back. I question myself, too. I just think I was in a place where I was so beaten down that I couldn't make good decisions for myself. I didn't feel good about myself. I think I felt ashamed and unworthy. All the emotions that keep you trapped in an unhealthy situation. After the sixth time I was kicked out and came back, I told him if it ever happened again, that was it; I would never come back. The seventh time, I walked out and closed that door for good.

After I left, he found my poetry, and I believe he burned it. I was devastated when I found out, at our divorce settlement, that he had destroyed forty years of my poetry writings. Although he never admitted to knowing anything. I had saved my poetry writings from the time before we were married and then all the writing that I had done for the seven years that we were together. When it was suggested by the two divorce attorneys that he take a lie detector test, he refused. It was decided by the attorneys that his refusal was as good as an admission of guilt. He had to pay $7,000 for the seven years we were married. I also eventually got my dog back. I had lived in fear every single day after I left that my dog was being abused by him.

I remember him saying things that made me afraid of what he was capable of or what he might have even done or been involved in. I was not sure if he was just saying things to scare me, if he was making it up, or if there was some truth to some of his stories. Like him telling me one time that he knew where a missing woman was and said that she was dead in a swamp. Or saying he understood the anger the person felt that went into a church and just started killing everybody. Big red flags. *Oh my God*, I thought, *how could this be?*

Mark had no care or concern for others. One day, while we were together in the car driving home, we passed by a house, and by the grace of God, I noticed that there was a small child in diapers who must have crawled out a window and was standing on the second-floor roof. I pointed it out to Mark, and with panic in my voice, I asked Mark to please stop the car and pull into the driveway. I was frantic and told him that I had to let the people who lived there know. I was terrified. We had to act fast. This very small child was in danger. But instead, Mark was telling me that I needed to mind my own business. This had nothing to do with us. I kept insisting and begging him to please stop. But instead, he kept driving, and he drove the rest of the way to our house. I could not believe it. As soon as he stopped the car, I swung open my door and told him that I was going to run to their house. We lived in the country, so this would be a good distance away. Finally, Mark yelled at me and told me to get back in the car, and he drove to their home. I ran as fast as I could to their front door, and I started wildly pounding on the door. The father answered, and he was a bit irritated, but of course, he had no idea why I was pounding so loud. I blurted out with a scared, shaky voice, "There is a small baby out on your roof." He immediately looked shocked and scared and started running up the stairs while yelling back, "My older daughter was supposed to be watching the baby." The dad was able to get there in time. I was so relieved that the baby was safe. It took me quite a while to calm back down. But I was in shock and disbelief that my husband absolutely did not care. He was perfectly okay with whatever happened. What kind of person was he that he could let a small child possibly fall to their death and not have any emotion about whether the child lived or died? He acted in the same manner and way as when my dad was sick. Mark could have cared less about what happened to my dad. He felt that I was married and belonged to him, and I did not need to be with my dad and visit him when he was sick.

Soon after I left, I found a wonderful women's group for therapy. I am continuing to attend and have joined other groups. It helps to be honest about your suffering. To try and move past it the best that you can. One of the important things that I have learned is the importance of boundaries. Abuse comes in a lot of different ways. I felt that I was Mark's puppet. He would pull my strings, and I was always under his complete control.

I have forgiven Mark. My faith gives me hope and strength to get by. People ask me how I could ever forgive him. But anger and hate are all-consuming. It is a poison to us. I have found that forgiveness releases you from that bondage. During those seven years, I suffered his abuse; I kept praying and believing. It is how I survived.

Having worked on myself, I know that growing up as a child, I was a people pleaser. I always tried to do what was right, but I never really felt like I was good enough. I had low self-esteem.

Before my mom died, she shared many wisdoms, but one that always stuck with me is, "If you shake the family tree enough, a lot of nuts will fall out," and, "Never ever talk about your dirty laundry."

Red flags, I ignored so many. When I look back now at the many excuses I created for both my first marriage and my second marriage, I truly feel foolish. Instead of flat out telling either husband that if their behavior continued, I would no longer be a part of their life. I didn't do that. Instead, my reaction was that I cried, and I blamed myself. The problems in both of my marriages, I believe, were because I put them on a pedestal. God asks us to put no other gods before him. I did that with both men.

I was so confused with Mark. One moment, he couldn't live without me; the next, he was vicious with rage, and I feared for my safety and my life.

It was much different with my second husband. I was so much in love with first husband that I was certain that I could not exist without him; I would most certainly just die. My life would be over. I was devastated, wondering and questioning how it was even possible that he did not care. How was it so easy for him to end our marriage and just let me go? For two years before our divorce, I was in counseling, hoping it would save our marriage. I told my counselor that I was afraid to ask him one simple question. That question was to ask my husband, the man that I loved and the father of our two sons, if he still wanted me in his life. My counselor said that when I felt strong enough, I could ask him that question. It took me two years before I had enough nerve to ask. One day, I finally asked. He did not give me an answer or even a response. His not answering me was his honest answer. So, there it was. We had been married for thirty-seven years, and he couldn't even answer.

We look at people on the outside and sometimes think their world seems perfect. I've learned over the years that, many times, this is so very far from the truth.

Don't be so quick to blame yourself for things that go wrong. And take time to listen to others and have compassion. Helping others helps our healing.

The positive that I can share about those seven years that I was married to my second husband is that it brought me closer to God, and I am also stronger. I look back at all that I endured and suffered, and I'm still here. I survived it. My genuine hope is that, by sharing my story, it might help others.

When you know what it feels like to live in darkness, finding the light and sharing the light with others becomes more important.

Chapter Nine:

Angels Are Messengers. I Listen Intently to the Messages

CASSANDRA'S INTERVIEW AND STORY.

There is a lot that I have learned over the past sixty-plus years of my life. Some of those years were good and there were a lot of years that were not particularly good at all. But the years that were the hardest for me, I consider them to be some of my best years, because they helped to shape me into the person that I am today. A person who cares about the quality of life not just for me, but also for others. And so, I live modestly and find joy in helping other people. I am passionate about helping in many ways. The kind of help that brings hope and healing for others.

We all come to a place or juncture at some time in our lives where we start to look at our true meaning and purpose. For me, that time of reflection about my life set me on a course and direction that I had never imagined or even thought of. I am still definitely a work in progress. And I hope there are many more years left in my life to enjoy and to be able to accomplish even more. But I am taking it one day at a time, getting up every day, and asking my spirit to help guide me.

My memory of my life as a little girl growing up is not filled with many happy memories, even though we didn't have to want for anything. My mother was a homemaker, and my father was an engineer and sales rep for a large and successful company. The company paid him a very good salary, and money was not a problem. We lived in upper New York. We lived together in a large house that my father built, and it was filled with lots of nice things. I had an older sister and brother and a brother that was younger than me. But what our very nice house and large family did not have was any love or affection. That simply did not exist between the walls of our house. When I would go to a friend's house, I thought it odd that their parents shared one room, as mine had their own rooms. Praise and encouragement were also absent in our home. Things were just a matter of fact. We would go to school, do our homework, practice piano, and do our chores; in retrospect, our house was run like it was a business. When I was young, I enjoyed my mom's company as she taught me to bake, sew, and do many kinds of crafts. But as I got older, that faded away, and my mom became more angry, bitter, and unfriendly. But there was also no love between us siblings. We never did anything together as a family. That is unless, on the rare occasion, that company or relatives were coming to visit. Then we all fell into our roles and played that we were just one big happy family. Those, to me, were fond memories but rare ones. I loved it when my favorite uncle came to visit. He treated me especially and always spoiled me when we went shopping. I remember overhearing an argument between him and my parents. My parents were mad because he bought me so many school clothes. He told them that they treated me like the forgotten kid, and the others always got more attention than I did, and he was just making up for that. Funny, I never felt that way. I was just grateful for any scrap of attention I did get.

So, it is very safe to say that we truly had no role models growing up. Not how to be a family, not how to treat your spouse.

My dad was an only child, and I learned later in life that my mom had a very tumultuous relationship with her family, which led us to living a rather solitary existence.

I was a shy, super-sensitive kid who lacked confidence and was very much a loner. I was a good little girl who just wanted people to like me, but I was picked on terribly by my family because I was so sensitive, and I cried easily. We lived out in the country, so the few friends I had I did not see very often. I spent an enormous amount of time by myself, playing outside or with our many family pets. There was one day I will never forget. While playing in the backyard, I looked back toward our house, and I asked myself, "Who are those people who live there? I feel like I don't belong here. Why am I here?" As I look back now to that time in my life, I now know that I was there for a reason. We were all there for a purpose.

Church and God were never prominent in our home. I do remember attending various churches: Episcopalian, Lutheran,

Methodist, Baptist, and Catholic. I was curious and enjoyed seeing the different religions, but we never consistently went for any length of time. I remember my mom dropping me off at church so I could play piano with the organist, but she never stayed for the service. Despite that, I always knew there was a higher power out there, though I never really felt connected to them. I always felt alone to fend for myself.

My parents split up and divorced when I was eleven. My sister was already on her own. Our younger three stayed with my mom. But that didn't last long; my brothers hated my mom's new boyfriend, and this constantly caused all kinds of trouble. It was not long before both left to live with my dad, leaving just me at home, which was soon put up for sale as my mom could not afford it now.

My mother's boyfriend was a fire chief who also owned the grocery store in our town. Being a very small town, the scandal of the fire chief leaving his wife and moving in with my mom was big news. The gossip was pretty debilitating for me. Rumors of the "cheating" while married were hard to hear, and worse, my mom became known as the town prostitute. That led to me being shunned and excluded from playdates, parties, and sleepovers. This was the 1960s, and you didn't associate with divorced mothers or their children. It just was not good to have your children be exposed to "that kind of people," as I was labeled. I remember my mom getting very bitter and angry. I remember her drinking. I am told that she drank before that time, but this is when I remember seeing it for myself.

By the time I began high school, I became more insecure and very awkward. I only had a couple of friends with whom I felt close. But certainly not cool enough to be invited to parties. I spent nearly every Friday and Saturday babysitting, learning the power of earning money. There was one girl in particular whose parents seemed to know that I needed some TLC (tender loving care) and often invited me on their family outings. Even so far as inviting me to Florida and a trip to Disney World. Sadly, as she became a cool girl, I was discarded. I was grateful when another divorced mom with a daughter my age moved into town. We became fast friends, but that, too, didn't last very long, as she was way more outgoing and made other friends who didn't like me.

Meanwhile, at my house, my mom seemed to be getting more agitated more often. I started to see a temper, and there was often yelling. My mother was never officially diagnosed, but there is a strong probability that she was bipolar, in addition to being extremely paranoid. She was constantly in everyone's business and accusing people of things that she thought they did. Especially her boyfriend; she was always accusing him of flirting. Whenever things escalated, he would give me a little wink and shush me out of the room so I would not have to be in the middle of anything. I loved my stepdad for that. He was one of the first people who acted like they cared about me. I have such fond memories of accompanying him to "Firemen Parades" every weekend of the summer. I would twirl baton as the band led our town's firefighters in parade after parade. He always acted so proud of me.

I had a boyfriend in high school. He was a popular kid, but I was not. He preyed on the fact that I had no self-esteem and bullied me often. Because of my being teased my whole childhood, I accepted his behavior as normal. He would call me names, tell me I was a prostitute like my mother, say I would never amount to anything, and, on a couple of occasions, hit me. Mom was especially critical of him but never offered any kind of motherly advice; it was always dismissive and accusatory. Even though we hadn't had sex, she had accused me of it. She felt because my sister had gotten pregnant in high school, I should be labeled that way as well. Since I was a teen, my reaction was, "Well, if my mom is accusing me of it, I might as well." I did not know any better. I never had any guidance. I was left to figure everything out all on my own. I didn't get everything right because I did not deserve him hitting me, accusing me, and calling me names. Which, sadly, led to more years of accepting horrible treatment like that from others.

Since the weekends of parades involved beer tents and rowdy firemen, my mom's drinking got heavier. It became a Saturday night ritual for her to be drunk and embarrass me in front of friends. Luckily, at sixteen, I got my license and gained great independence. The day of my birthday I was taken to the bank by my dad to get a car loan to buy my first car. Not given a car like my siblings but given a car payment. The day after my sixteenth birthday, I started working at a local mall. I loved working and made lots of new friends who were from other towns, who didn't know anything about me and took me for who I was, not my family. I graduated from high school at the age of seventeen. I knew my mom and stepdad wanted to move to Florida, and so that pushed me to move quicker with my decision to move out. A week after high school, I had my own apartment.

My real father had never been warm and fuzzy with me, and I had not spent much time with him after the divorce. And besides, he had his hands full with his new wife, her daughter, and my little brother, who was a handful. It was not until I became an adult that I got to know my stepmom. She and I are friends to this day.

It had been assumed by everyone in my family that I would not be going to college. My father, having paid for my brother and sister to go to college only to have them quit, decided that I was not worth the effort and was advised to look for secretary work. I was a good student, had good grades, and knew I wanted more out of life. But with no support and no resources, it didn't seem hopeful. I applied to a business trade school, took an application test, and was awarded a scholarship. My family and high school were mad at me because I never told them about the school or the scholarship. I figured, why bother? No one acted like they cared. I learned at my high school graduation that someone at the school did care. As I said, I was a quiet girl but loved to work hard. One of our class advisors stood up at graduation and talked about how hard I worked and never asked for or got any recognition. He awarded me a hundred-dollar scholarship.

I was so touched you would have thought he gave me a million dollars. I will never forget him. And now, every year, through my business, I award a graduating senior an "Unsung Hero Scholarship."

After finishing trade school at nineteen, I worked in retail and quickly earned myself some promotions, becoming an assistant manager of a clothing store. I loved work; for once, I felt good about myself.

Soon after graduation, my sister, who was married and living in New Jersey, reached out to me and asked if I wanted to come and live with her. It sounded like a way to not be all alone and maybe have some better opportunities far away from the small, hurtful town I grew up in. I made the move to New Jersey. But shortly after arriving, I found out that my sister only wanted me there because she was getting a divorce from her husband. She needed me so she could afford to leave her husband and have someone help share the rent. We rented a little house and had lots of adventures. It felt nice for once to have a big sister. But in due time, I learned that she was a master at manipulating people for her gain. I was always her partner when she wanted to go pick up men at the bar, buy something she couldn't afford, and just do something she didn't want to do. On one double date with twins, the brother who was my date forced himself on me sexually. Without having my consent and without stopping, even though I kept pleading. Later that night, when I told her because she found me sobbing incoherently on his doorstep, she was barely remorseful, almost shaming me for not being more worldly about men. My sister never watched over me, nor did she watch out for me. I was just a tool that she needed for her plans, needs, and wants, and at the time, I was too naïve to know any better.

I remember one day when my dad was singing her praises, I tried to tell him about the rape, but he simply said he did not want to hear about it. He always defended her and always sang her praises. I never remember getting praised.

All of us kids were smart. One time, when I was in the tenth grade at school, I showed my dad a paper from school, and that I had scored a 99 out of 100 on a state exam. He said to me, "Well, then you must have made a stupid mistake, you should have gotten 100." That hurt, but it made me even more determined that for the next year, I would get 100. I proudly showed him that I had scored one hundred correct answers. But he had nothing to say at all. I wanted to at least hear him say, "Good job," but all I got was silence. Ouch, that hurt. But I walked away that day, and I said to myself, "Okay, Dad…now I am even more determined." I never held that against him. I always just accepted the crumbs people gave me. I guess I didn't know any better and probably didn't think I deserved any better.

My sister's next great scheme was to run off to Florida and marry husband number three. Thus, leaving me alone to fend for myself in the house that we had rented together and that I could not afford on my own. At the company where I worked, there was a guy who was fourteen years older than me, and I knew he had a crush on me. He was divorced, with three kids whom he had on the weekends. We had a couple of dates before my sister left, and when I told him what happened, he told me he would help. We stayed in the rental house for a few months, and then I moved in with him. Though honestly, I was not prepared to move in with a man fourteen years older. I adored his children; they were two, four, and six, and we quickly bonded. Two years later, we were married. The kids and I shared so many great times. I finally had the family I always longed for.

My job was going very well, and I had received more than one promotion. But my marriage was starting to not go so well. It seemed the more confidence I got in myself, the more my husband started turning on me. He complained about everything. My cooking, my cleaning, and even if the freezer was out of ice. I thought things would be better if I made changes. I started begging to move out to the country. We bought a home on twenty acres and filled it with lots of animals and toys for the kids. I lived for the weekends when I could play with the kids; he lived for the weekends when he could play golf.

It was also soon after we were married when an emergency surgery for severe abdominal pain revealed that I had endometriosis. A condition that I spent over twenty years battling. I tried drugs to combat its growth, but the drugs all had such bad side effects that I did not want to take them. My only solution was surgery. Over the next eighteen years, I had nine surgeries to detach organs that had become fused and, lastly, to remove an ovary. I remember his total lack of concern for my well-being. Most surgeries were on the same day, and I can recall several times the nurses had to make multiple calls to have him come pick me up. Once, when I needed a hospital stay, the nurse found me in tears because, for two days, he did not come to see me or bring the kids to visit me. She called him and reprimanded him because the next day, he dropped the kids off in my hospital room and left to play golf. I was exhausted and upset when he got back five hours later. When I tried to explain to him it was "too much for me," he just snapped at me and said, "Well, *you* wanted to see them."

I just did not understand why he treated me so badly. To everyone else, he was kind and friendly, but behind closed doors, he was cruel and manipulative. Everything was always on his terms. He would tell me to get all the kids in the car; we needed to leave. Then he proceeded to wash the car while we all sat in a hot car waiting for him. I would always make it a joke to the kids, but inside of me, I was hurt. I remember one time, I had one of our tractor wagons fall on my foot, and I needed to go to the ER. He reluctantly took me, grumbling all the way, and even slammed the door to the ER in my face as I followed in behind him. Again, I didn't know better and just accepted what crumbs he gave me. Years later, when the kids were in their teens, they would say, "Why are you still with him if he treats you horribly?"

After being married for six years, I now longed for a baby of my own, and it was highly suggested by my doctor to help suppress the endometriosis growth. He did not want another child, but he finally agreed. Secretly, I thought he would love me more if I gave him a baby. We had a baby girl who he adored, and in my mind, things were going to be okay.

It was not long after that my mom and stepdad got divorced. She was distraught and scared to be alone, so I invited her to move in with us. It was a nightmare from day one. I had not really spent much time with her over the years, just an occasional visit or phone call, but I soon realized her paranoia and drinking were much worse. She was constantly accusing everyone about one thing after another and taking everything out on me. My husband had no patience with her, and I was in the middle of a mess, so I convinced her she better go back to Florida, where I knew she would be much happier.

Soon after our daughter was born, his youngest moved in with us, too. She was a sweet kid but had lots of scars from her childhood at her mom's. And I soon learned of other horrible scars.

When we moved, his father moved to the country with us. I never really liked him and never really knew why. He always bought me expensive gifts, which made me feel uncomfortable. My husband would dismiss it, saying I should be more appreciative. Through a series of circumstances, I discovered that my husband's father had been molesting the three older children. The oldest girl was sixteen, and the youngest was ten when I found out, and it had been going on for years. How could I not know this? My intuition was telling me something was bad about him, but I did not listen. I felt so guilty. When I told my husband, I said that he had a choice that he had to make. Either he made his dad move out, or I was leaving him. He agreed to make his father leave, but he would not pursue the issue any further. In other words, he would not accept any responsibility for dealing with his children's hurt or suffering. This was unfathomable to me. How could a father be so heartless? I was truly heartbroken.

I had started some consulting work when our daughter was first born so that I could be at home with her. This was going well for me, but being home gave me more time to think about how unhappy I was in my marriage. I still wanted to have another baby, but honestly, I was not sure I wanted it with him, so I began looking into adoption. He desired to move, as he no longer liked the responsibility of twenty acres, and quite honestly, I was happy to move to a better school system. I did not like the house he insisted we buy, but he did, and to appease him, I said yes. One of the companies that I was consulting with offered me a full-time position. It was a nice offer, a great offer, so I took it. At this point, my work was providing me with the opportunity for a lot of self-growth, and my confidence grew every day. I was lucky to have great bosses who pushed me to learn a lot and grow. With that newfound confidence, I gave him six months to make things better between us, or I would leave. Over the next six months, nothing changed. He was nasty to me, and he resented me. If I came home later from work, he would greet me with a comment like, "What did you screw up today that made you late?" He said he did not love me. I had enough. I was turning forty and determined to have a better life. I found a place near my job, and for the first time in years, I felt free from constant complaining and harassment. I finally felt at peace. I just knew that everything was going to be okay for my daughter and me. But there was one thing that I still very much wanted, and that was a baby.

I had a friend who kept bugging me about moving to Ohio, so that was on my radar. I knew that with my resume, I could get a good job rather easily. I started telling people about my plan and remembered talking to one of our vendors at work, asking if he knew anything about Columbus. A couple of weeks later, he needed me to sign a contract. He sat in front of me and said these words I will never forget: "Please don't go to Columbus. I have loved you since the moment I saw you. Please, stay so I can get to know you." Oh, Wow, what is a girl supposed to say to that? Of course, I stayed, and we soon started dating. Only one problem: I still desperately wanted another baby. Soon to be forty, I did not want to wait. He begged me to wait; he wanted to marry me, and he wanted the baby to be his.

The next eighteen months that we dated felt like a fairytale to me. He loved my daughter and was the kindest, most loving man to me. We had so much fun together I could not imagine being any happier.

Not quite a year after we married, my husband's ex-wife suddenly died, and his two children, ages thirteen and seven, came to live with us. Their mom was supposed to be homeschooling them, but it was clear she seldom taught them anything. The seven-year-old had no education and barely knew numbers or letters. Because they did not go to school and only left the house to attend church twice a week, they had no rules, no bedtime, and no dinner time. Their behavior was that of wild animals. They ate what and when they wanted and slept when and where they wanted. My house had rules, and they wanted no part of that. They also had not received any medical treatment for years because of religious beliefs. His ex-wife had died from an aneurysm that she knew she had, but because of her beliefs, she did not seek treatment. His girls blamed me for the divorce and, subsequently, their mother's death. They had no respect for me and treated me and my daughter horribly, and my husband let them.

From that moment on, my husband became a different person. I'm sure it had something to do with guilt regarding his ex-wife's death, but all I know is my fairy tale had just become a nightmare. His loving nature with me was no longer displayed, or his girls would become jealous. He no longer gave my daughter any attention, or his girls would become jealous. When she tried to speak up for herself, he told her to "get over it, their mother just died." I remember so many times when I would try to hold his hand while walking somewhere, and his youngest would come between us and take our hands apart, and he let her.

The year his wife died was just the beginning of one of the hardest years of my life. Thinking back, I am not even sure how we did it. My best friend's son took his own life, and then a friend of my daughter's was killed in an auto accident. Her once-loving stepdad not only wanted nothing to do with her but allowed his kids to treat her badly. She was seventeen years old; this was all too much for her, and she sank into a deep depression. Anti-depressants for teens were becoming rather common, so her doctor prescribed them. The result was an even deeper depression and her trying to hurt herself. Thank God, I found her and rushed her to the ER. It was in that ER that my life soon took another hit. The ER doctor came to me and said, "Did you know your daughter has a rare heart condition?" Her heart had too many electrodes. This is the condition where young athletes will drop dead on the field with no warning.

The next several months were a blur. The girls were forced to go to school, but my husband caved to their constant complaining and let them skip constantly. That angered me and my daughter who did not understand the new division of rules in the house. The whole situation also angered my sister, who had moved back from Florida several years ago. She never had any children and could not understand why I was not giving her more attention. It's fair to say our relationship ended when she yelled at me while I was sitting in the ER with my daughter and refused to take her to her doctor's appointment to tend to a broken foot she suffered in a drunken fall.

Through all this, my daughter became more depressed and now scared for her life. Daily, I would pick her up from school because she thought her heart was beating wrong. It was just too much for her to think she was a ticking time bomb and again tried to hurt herself. I had no choice but to commit her to a facility for a week of observation. It was one of the hardest decisions I had to make, but luckily it saved her life. It was like a wake-up call to be with other teens who also were going through so much. I believe her compassion for those kids saved her.

We also decided to go ahead with the "somewhat risky," as we were told, procedure to determine the severity of her heart condition. We learned that while her condition was dangerous, with constant monitoring, they didn't feel she was in any immediate danger.

And I believe there was another miracle that saved us. Amidst all this chaos, I became pregnant. After years of trying, I had concluded that my endometriosis was not going to let it happen. But lo and behold, I was pregnant at forty-four.

Of course, when my second daughter was born, the whole town gossiped that they thought it must have been my oldest daughter's baby, and that was why she had missed so much school.

Life was a bit calmer in my new daughter's early years, and we settled into a very dysfunctional way of life with no choice but to make it work. My husband grew increasingly distant and often had weeklong bouts of depression that he cured with alcohol and sleep. I was very hurt about my husband's behavior and unhappy about the way he and my stepdaughters treated me and my older daughter, so I poured myself into my consulting career and raising my new little one. My older daughter went off to college, so I felt comfortable taking a consulting job with a company in Ohio that allowed me to travel and escape the horrors of my household.

It seems that when my life got the least bit comfortable for me, the Spirit decided to give me another wake-up call. Years ago, I had fallen and hurt my wrist, and I had constant nerve pain that I needed to address. Surgery to repair the nerves left me with a life-threatening infection. The doctor who did the surgery would not believe me, and it was not until my arm became septic that I was sent for treatment. This resulted in years of complications, as the infection had caused bone damage. I was bounced from doctor to doctor because no one wanted to treat me for an injury they knew was caused by another doctor. I remember the day I met the doctor that saved my hand. My husband was in "one of his depressions" and refused to take me to the appointment. It was hard to handle the baby and drive with one arm. So, my older daughter drove us. As the doctor had explained later, I was close to needing it amputated. He performed several surgeries where he was able to rebuild some bones and then fuse my wrist.

In the middle of this mess, my husband slowly fell deeper and deeper into depression. I felt alone and helpless and tried what little I could to get him out of it. He loved home repair and working with his hands, so I thought having a big project to work on would make him feel better. So, we bought a fixer-upper that my older daughter and friends lived in while we worked on it. Needless to say, he did virtually nothing to the home.

His family refused to believe he needed help and suggested I was exaggerating. My friends did not offer any help or support, either. I remember confiding in my best friend, asking her if I could name her in my will, that if anything happened to me, she would take care of my two girls. She flat-out told me she did not want to be involved.

My husband then began to complain about neck pain and was told he needed surgery. Not three weeks later, I was hospitalized for an emergency hysterectomy. I spent a week in the hospital due to complications from the surgery that resulted in a blood clot in my leg. The next three months were unbearable, dealing with medication and its side effects for the blood clot. Thank goodness, it dissolved, and thank goodness for my daughter, who took care of me and the baby.

At this point, my husband became dependent not only on his alcohol but also on oxycodone, which was prescribed after his first surgery. It was a vicious cycle of him complaining of pain, getting more drugs, and finding a doctor to do more operations. When I confronted one of his doctors to tell him that I believed he was abusing the drugs and washing them down with a bottle of wine every night, the doctor's response was, "I guess you married the wrong man, didn't you?" *Again*, I thought, *is it me who just doesn't understand?*

It was probably a year or so later when, again, I was sucker-punched by the universe. While feeding my daughter's horses, one of the new rescue horses kicked me in the chest and sent me flying into the fence. I crawled into her house and called 911. I remember lying on the ground outside the sliding door, praying for strength to open the door and praying for my life to be spared. I believe it was my beloved stepdad, who had recently died, who gave me the strength to open the door and helped me inside.

I spent a week in the hospital where, after hours of surgery, they found my gall bladder was torn from my liver. I spent the next three months mostly bedridden. I needed a wheelchair to get around because walking was so painful. I would do my consulting work from my bed because we could not afford for me not to work.

At this point, my husband was barely functioning. He would skip work as often as his kids would skip school. He slept for hours at a time on the couch, and honestly, there was very little I could do in my condition.

I begged him to take care of things, pay bills, and make important phone calls, but I learned that none of that was getting done. It was Valentine's weekend when I finally felt I could spend more than one day at a time out of my bed. I decided I needed a little break and went to New City to visit my cousin. I took the baby, who was now four, and we had a wonderful time feeling pampered by my cousin. I returned on Sunday night to my husband and his eighteen-year-old daughter having a screaming match. I learned that he had "taken all of her alcohol from her room" and drank it all. That was the last straw. I told him to leave the house now. His youngest started screaming at me, and I said, "You need to go, too." I turned to the older daughter and said, "What is your choice? Stay here with my rules, or leave, too?" She asked to stay.

I spent the next few days tearing the house apart. I found empty bottle after empty bottle of alcohol. Pill bottles tucked behind rafters in the garage and behind plumbing under sinks. And to top it off, two large tubs of unopened mail. He did nothing while I was recuperating. Bills were all in arrears, and the two houses were in foreclosure.

I think I was in total shock. I had no idea where to turn and was scared, ashamed, and extremely overwhelmed. Comments from friends and family were shameful. "How could you let this happen?" "I can't believe you didn't see this coming!"

It was at this lowest point in my life that, for the first time in my life, I became aware of the angels who kept showing themselves to me and whom I kept dismissing as unimportant. Now, I was bombarded with them and was forced to take notice. My hairdresser, a casual friend, called me at home and talked for hours about his life and how he understood what I was going through. He not only gave me good advice but a shoulder to lean on if I ever needed it. A parent of my daughter's friend stepped up, helped me with desperate home repairs, and even paid for my young daughter to attend summer camp, giving me a well-deserved break. The attorney my hairdresser recommended was so compassionate. And I will never forget the bank teller who took a lot of extra time to give me great advice when I approached her in tears about bounced checks. These angels will be added to my list and never forgotten. My favorite uncle, my stepdad, my girlfriend's parents, the teacher at graduation, the doctor who saved my hand, and, most importantly, my daughters.

The next year was spent trying to clean up this mess and finding a future. I was starting over from completely zero in my fifties, and I had nowhere to go but up. For some reason, I was blessed with a great work ethic and blind determination, so I put them both to work for me.

I had a good friend in Ohio at the company I consulted for who begged me to come live there. She even said I could live in the family's rental property while I figured things out. Having traveled there so much, I felt comfortable and thought of it as a stopping point on the way to a future in a warmer climate.

So, my younger daughter and I packed a six-bedroom home in New Jersey into a two-bedroom bungalow in Ohio and started to heal. I spent the next year very quiet and introspective. I did consulting work from my couch and created a comfy little nest for the two of us. My husband was going from bad to worse; he lived with his mom, and she just enabled all his addictions. His mom even blamed me so much that she convinced him to take my name off from being a beneficiary of his retirement savings.

After I learned he had had several car accidents, I knew I should divorce him. I truly did not want to. Through all of this, I still felt love for him. But I feared he would kill someone on the road, and we would be sued. My life was finally calming down; I needed to protect myself and my daughter.

He died several months later from an overdose. I was heartbroken. In my head, I kept saying, "When he hits rock bottom, he will get better and come back to us." That was never going to happen, and now I had to figure out my future all by myself. That chapter needed to end.

A few months before my husband's death, my father was diagnosed with colon cancer. Being in his eighties, he refused treatment and passed within a couple of weeks of my husband. I was kind of numb to my dad's death. He was not a strong force in my life, but I respected him nonetheless and recognized his tough love made me who I am today.

My focus was then on what I would do to take care of my daughter and me and, at the same time, provide for my future since I was in my fifties and had lost everything. Years of exhausting my savings to help step-kids go to college and not asking for any money from my first husband after divorcing had put me in a scary spot financially. At this point, I felt very stuck, and the thought of moving again, even to a warmer climate, felt extra scary.

My older daughter, who had recently married, would come visit me in Ohio. Her life was leading her and her new husband to Silicon Valley in California, but when they saw how inexpensive life was in the Midwest, they decided to buy a house forty-five minutes north of where I lived. Soon after, they had a son, and I knew at this point that I would never move far from them; in fact, I wanted to be closer. So, this new little angel that just came into the world was changing my life again. I was developing a plan to create a little store where I lived. A shop filled with things I loved: coffee, baked goods, crafts, and ice cream. I did not have a dime, but I had a dream, and that's all that mattered.

I was pretty shy about my dream and only told my daughters, but they have always supported me no matter what. One day, when we were exploring, we found a vacant old church in a quaint small town that I quickly fell in love with. My daughters and I toured the inside, and though we were extremely overwhelmed by the years of clutter left by the former owners of a daycare, the building emitted a genuine feeling of love and warmth. I did not know how I was going to buy it, but I knew it was mine. I kept running into obstacles trying to buy the property but convinced the owner to let me rent until I figured it out.

When my older daughter moved to Ohio, her dad, my first husband, would often come and visit. He knew what happened to my second husband and was genuinely kind and caring. I was very hesitant to accept any of his charity toward me, but he absolutely adored my younger daughter and loved to spoil her rotten just like he did her big sister. I was happy that she had a hero in her life and let him be a part of ours. There were several times when he asked me to marry him again, but I just couldn't; I didn't love him. During one of his visits, I expressed my desire to buy the old church and how I kept hitting roadblocks with realtors and banks. Not only did he offer to give me the money, but he went on to explain that I had asked for nothing in our marriage or divorce, and he knew that he treated me badly. He said that I was such a good wife and mom, and I deserved so much better, and he wanted to give me the money to buy the church. I was shocked and naturally just could not accept it; I wasn't used to people just giving me things. After much discussion, I agreed to take the money on the condition that I pay it back in the form of college savings for our daughter's children.

Right after I purchased the church, my younger brother from New York reached out to me. He heard about my husband's death and offered condolences, but as I learned later, he needed me more. He was down on his luck after a double hip replacement, separated from his wife, and needed a friend. I told him I now lived in a large church with plenty of room, and he was welcome to come and help me renovate it. Another lesson was coming my way. Seems my brother was an alcoholic who was filled with anxiety and depression. Over eighteen months, I checked him into rehab twice, only to have him check himself out. At that point, I needed him out of my house. I was not equipped to handle his problems, and it was too reminiscent of dealing with my husband to have him near me and my daughter. I got him a job and set him up in an apartment down the street. I would get frequent calls when he needed money, and when I started refusing, he got nasty with me. He would sit out front of his apartment and flip me off when I drove by. I would laugh and sometimes do it back. Months went by that we hadn't spoken when he contacted me to help take him to the hospital. He was very sick with smoking and drinking-related conditions, and I knew at this point he didn't have long to live. I helped him up until the time he died, and then my family helped empty and clean his apartment, which was the filthiest I've ever seen.

Little by little, with every bit of money I could save each month, I worked on converting the church from a daycare back to its place of honor, once again a lovely place where people gather for a little peace, a little kindness, and a sense of community.

I was still shy about telling people what I wanted to do but soon learned that once I did, the project took on a life of its own. I was witnessing the "Law of Attraction" in full force. Everyone wanted to help. Nearly every fixture in my store was donated to me. I decided to sell goods on consignment so I would not have to outlay any money, and merchandise started coming in by the truckload as donations. My new Ohio friends were donating their time, and my dream was becoming a reality. I was suddenly both pushed and driven by an unknown force.

Through the years, my mom remained in my life in a small way. Her bipolar, paranoid behavior would spike every couple of months as I would get calls with her yelling or crying about someone doing something to her. Or calls from her landlord about her drunken behavior. I became more and more detached and tried to laugh it off. She drank daily, and I knew never to call after five, or it would end in a fight. I was grateful we lived over a thousand miles apart, although I was very bitter that my brother and his family would ignore her, even though they lived five minutes from her. No, she wasn't the best parent, but she was clearly mentally ill. Her life seemed so troubled I grew to have empathy for her, and I would pray for her constantly and wish her peace. I shopped for her weekly to make sure she had everything she needed delivered to her. A few months ago, at ninety-three, she was hospitalized, and they discovered she had a large aortic aneurysm. She was put in hospice care and sent home to live her life out. I visited her and would talk to her often. She would not admit she had anything wrong with her, and I respected and tried to do everything she asked of me. Her final wishes were that no family be told of her passing. She passed a few weeks ago, and I honored that. May she finally have found peace.

I've spent the last several years trying to make sense of all that has happened in my life and, most recently, mourning the loss of a mother I never really felt I had. To this day, I wish I had a mom to have a mother-daughter talk with. I still struggle with the loss of my second husband. I have trouble comprehending how and why he chose the life he did ahead of me and his daughters. My first husband has also passed, but I am grateful for the time we had before he passed and thankful for his apology and generosity.

I try not to dwell on the past because I know I'm here in my little coffee shop in my small town, spreading healing in every way I know how. I know so well what loneliness, not feeling love, and feelings of unworthiness feel like. I have also learned to be proud of myself for my strength and independence because no one has ever had my back; I have truly gone through this on my own. It is apparent now that angels have appeared so many times in my life to help me; it is now my time to give back.

Giving hugs to recent widows. Making friendly conversation with strangers who I can just tell are having a bad day. Talking with teens about finding their passion and not being discouraged by others who make assumptions about them. Counseling stepparents about troubles at home. Paying it forward with free ice cream cones to the kids who do good deeds or just need a smile. Sponsoring events for the town, working with local charities... this is all part of my day now.

I love every minute of being in my store. It has provided me with a purpose when I needed direction, it has helped me focus on others instead of myself, and it has absolutely brought me great healing. It is a privilege for me, every day, to keep this mission growing. To see and experience the positive impact that it is making in the community and for the many people who pass through the doors. Hope and healing reside inside.

But beyond a shadow of a doubt, I know I'm exactly where I am meant to be right now, and I wake up every day with excitement for the future. And I also know with absolute certainty that there are angels here in the rafters of this old church that constantly watch over me and my family of customers.

For others who have shared their life stories, many of them have suffered much worse. But together, we are all stronger just because we know that we are not facing it all alone.

DISCARDED

I thought him loving and kind

I thought he was quite a find

Later, I thought I'd go out of my mind

I believed his words of Love, how he couldn't be without me

Yet he told me from the start that someday, we'd probably part

Stories of his past, how others didn't last

His stories made certain I knew it could happen to me, too

I could be discarded…thrown away

I was disheartened, yet I stayed

I wanted the man with whom I fell in love

Not the one who thought he was above

Above the rules

Everyone else to him was fools

He was raging most of the time or wallowing in self-pity

He had a way of telling me that he was very, very witty

I remember being confused about how could he misconstrue.

He'd twist and turn my words. I was shocked at how often it oc-

curred

Without me, he said he'd fall apart

Moments later, again it would start

I couldn't seem to do anything right, day or night

He demanded that I leave…I cried…I grieved

The seventh time, I stayed away

I couldn't keep crawling back to another attack

Discarded and out the door

Why did I keep going back for more?

BH

Chapter Ten:

Eating Onion Sandwiches in the Desert

OLIVIA'S INTERVIEW AND STORY.

I was born in 1957 in a small city located on the southern shore of Lake Superior, which is in the Upper Peninsula of Michigan. As I reflect on my life growing up, I can say without hesitation that my life was filled with years of craziness and heartbreak. At the age of sixteen, I was so unhappy and feeling so desperate that I thought there was only one thing left that I could do. I had to move out. I had to get away. There had to be a better life out there for me.

For the first fifteen years of my life, before I turned sixteen, the craziness and heartbreak were what I knew and experienced almost every day. For the things I could not remember from my early childhood, my siblings and others helped to fill in the gaps. I wanted to know as much as possible. It helped me to understand more about myself and where I came from.

I'm beginning my story with my earliest memory: I am a little girl sitting at the kitchen table. I am eating puffed rice and puffed wheat cereal in a bowl that is filled with water, not milk. And instead of toast with my cereal, I have an onion sandwich. I have an older brother and sister, and for us, this was our daily meal for lunch and dinner. Closely connected to this time, I have another memory of my siblings and myself being secretly moved across the country, from the state of Michigan all the way to Las Vegas, Nevada. We were on the run. That is because my mother had just kidnapped my older brother, my sister, and me. These memories that I have are all tied together. That is, the memory of having no money, being on the run, and eating my cereal with water and onion sandwiches.

I often think back to that time, living in our tar-papered shack in the desert of Las Vegas with our mom. Today, if I am around even the faintest smell of tar, it immediately takes me back to that time and place. I picture myself as a little girl walking hand in hand with my mom, my sister, and my brother down a dark tar road, making our way back to our tar-papered shack in the desert.

Before being kidnapped by my mother and secretly moved to Las Vegas, there were a lot of twists and turns that caused my mom to make this bold and risky decision. By doing this, she had put herself at great risk for what she felt she had to do for the sake of her children. She could have faced jail time for kidnapping and crossing state lines.

My mother's name is Joy, and my father's name is Roger. My father made his living working as a merchant marine. My father had three children from a previous relationship before he married my mom. My father had two girls and a boy with a Native American woman who was from the Ojibwa tribe. It was after she died that my father met and married my mother. Together, they had

154

three children. Two girls and a boy, and I am the youngest girl. So, all together, my mother and father were raising six children.

I was born at home and delivered by my twelve-year-old half-sister. My dad was not home on the day I was born because he was working. He was out on the lakes at the time, so it was not possible for him to be there. I am so thankful that I have in my possession a rare and treasured photo from the day that I was born. In the photo, my older half-sister is holding me, and my siblings are all gathered around my mother.

I have learned a little bit about what a merchant marine's job is. I was told that my dad made a very good living doing it. During peace times, a merchant marine assists the navy in both refueling and cargo deliveries. His work was important, and he really loved what he did.

My mother came from a wealthy and prominent family that lived on the East Coast in New York City. My mother suffered from bipolar disorder all her life. When she was in the "high" stage of the disorder, she could become sexually promiscuous, and she also acted out. At a young age, her parents, after struggling with her antics, decided to send her away to an all-girls school in Wisconsin. While attending school there, she met and became involved with a man, and she ended up getting pregnant. Her parents, upon hearing this news, found themselves at their breaking point. It was told to me that between all her years of antics, her bipolar disorder, and then a pregnancy, her parents decided that this was all that they could take from her. They made the decision to disown her completely and legally. It seems harsh, but I feel that I cannot judge them or question their decision. There could be so much more that happened that forced them to have to make that decision. My mom decided to marry the father of her baby. It was not until recently that I was able to find out that her first husband, who fathered their child, was from Ohio. They ended up having two children, and their names were Susan and Alice.

My mom always worked herself to death. I believe the major reason for her doing that was because she was used to having wealth. At times, she would work two or three jobs when she was in her "high" phase of bipolar disorder. At one point, she even worked on the Alaskan pipeline because she could make very good money, even though it was considered hard work for a woman. She really wanted to regain that comfortable life that she had known and lived because of her parents. She had traveled all over the world as a young girl and had experienced some of the very finest things in life.

All my mother's extreme obsessions and her bipolar illness deeply affected her children. Our lives over the course of time, where my mother was concerned, were traumatic. When she was feeling good, she was good, but when she was suffering the downside of bipolar, she was bad, and then it was not good for anyone. It was scary to even be around her.

Shortly after I was born, my mother was called away to New York due to the death of her aunt. My father traveled to New

York with her. Her aunt was very wealthy and was fond of my mother. Because of the aunt's fondness, she bequeathed to my mother a large inheritance. For whatever reasons, which we were never told, my dad took full advantage of the situation. It is still shocking to me, but he decided to have my mom legally committed to an institution for the mentally insane. Next, he somehow took complete control of her inheritance. That wasn't enough; he didn't stop there. My father never returned home to us kids in Michigan. He utterly and completely abandoned all six of his children. Who does that? I have asked myself this question over and over again. Our father never called. He never checked up on us; he just left us there alone and on our own.

When the state found out about our situation, all six of us children became wards of the state. Until we could be placed in adequate care that met the state's qualifications, we were taken in by a lady named Kespie, who was a friend of my mother's. She was a native American woman, and she was very kind. She was also well known in the area for teaching women how to swim in Lake Superior. Kespie would swim in the frigid lake waters well into the cold month of November, attesting to her strong passion and deep love of the sport.

My older half-brother and half-sisters were taken and placed in an orphanage in Bay City, Michigan. My full-blooded sister and brother were sent to a foster home, and I was placed in a different foster home. My foster family were the McWilliams. While I have no memory of this time in my life, I am told that I was in pretty bad shape when they got me. I was dirty, malnourished, and I would not speak or play. I was told that I was about fifteen months old at the time. I also have no memory of the time when my mother was committed to the institution.

My mother's friend Kespie was heartbroken about what had happened to my mother and her children, and so, sometime later, she decided that she had to do something about it. She wrote a truthful and passionate letter to the judge explaining the situation and the true and factual details about what my father had done. She explained that my mother had not done anything wrong and that she had not abandoned her children. Thankfully, the judge proceeded to further investigate the matter. At the conclusion of the investigation, the judge ruled in my mother's favor. My mother was granted visits with her children from that time forward. He also allowed my mother to have planned outings with her children.

During my time with my foster family, they told my mother that they would very much like to adopt me. My mother told them that she could see how well-adjusted and happy I was, so she would allow it. She had no objections; she would agree to it. The McWilliams were happy and hopeful that she had given her approval, and so they proceeded with the petition to the court, but the court denied them. The reason the court gave for the denial was because of the frequent visits that my natural mother had with us. The court felt there was a strong presence in my life with my natural mother. As soon as my mom heard that the adoption was turned down, she went to work on a plan to get her kids back.

She made a bold plan. She made prior arrangements with both foster families to be allowed to take her three kids on an outing. She packed her car and picked us up just like there was nothing out of the ordinary about this day. But unbeknownst to them and us kids, we were on the run. Our destination was Las Vegas. My mom was indeed a very smart woman. She knew that there was no extradition between the states. Actually, my mom was often described as being a borderline genius, which is also a trait of bipolar disorder. She always seemed to be able to find a way to accumulate money when she needed it. So, she had money, a car, her kids, and a plan. We were on the run, and we were about to start a new life together more than two thousand miles away in Las Vegas, Nevada.

I only have limited memories of my mom visiting us while we were in foster care. But I do have some good memories that will bring a smile to my face about our time living in Las Vegas. After we first moved there, I was told that I would not speak at all. I was also told that this went on for a very long time. I was in a state of shock with all that had taken place, being kidnapped and moved to a strange new place. But then, little by little, I started to come out of my quiet, safe place. I was told that I became quite the little stinker. They described me at this time as a little pistol.

My mother insisted that we kids had to call her Momma Joy.

Momma Joy worked as a cocktail waitress for one of her jobs, and I think she stowed us away sometimes in the back room of where she worked. I have some flashbacks of how to "make a glass sing" and some other little bar antics. Then, my Momma Joy met a man. They married, and so then we had a new father, and we called him "Daddy Bob." I absolutely adored Daddy Bob, and I feel that he adored me, too. I have lots of memories of him carting me around on his shoulders. He was so good to us. As a family, we would go to parades, where I saw clowns for the very first time, walking around on stilts. I thought that the clowns were just really tall and had really long legs. One time, Daddy Bob was put in a "charity jail" to raise money for a particular charity. I had no idea what a charity jail was, and so I was completely distraught. I was crying that my Daddy Bob was locked up. He had captured my heart, and I did not want to lose him. I loved him. I sobbed and sobbed over this.

A few years later, my mother became sick again. My mother's dark times were upon us. When these episodes happened, she could be terribly abusive to everyone. She would go into one of her destructive episodes, and we would all live in fear of what might possibly happen. She knew that she was at a breaking point. So, she put us kids and herself all on a private plane, and we flew back to Detroit, Michigan. Because my mom had grown up privileged, a private plane was not a stretch for her. She had sailed on the *Queen Mary* and had attended an elite all-girls private school. She knew how to get around.

I remember being on the plane, curled up next to my mom, and looking out the window and seeing below on the ground all these tiny, little, what I thought were toy cars. I remember pointing to them and telling my mother to look out her window to see what I was seeing. I asked her if I could have one, and she looked down at me and smiled. It was Christmas Eve, the day we celebrate the birth of Jesus, a happy time for most families and children. However, little did I know that our mother was taking her children to be dropped off and returned to the adoption agency. On this very sad Christmas Eve memory, I am four years old.

When we landed at the airport in Michigan and we were making our way through the parking lot, my mom looked down at me and asked if I still wanted one of those toy cars that I saw from the plane. I immediately recognized my error about what I thought I saw from inside the plane when I saw my mother's wry smile on her face. Next, we all piled into a taxi. As I am sitting next to my mother, I'm tugging on her and asking her if I can please have a furry rabbit when we get to wherever it is she is taking us.

Our mom attempted to drop us off in front of the house of the man who was the head of the Lutheran Children's Friend Society, Mr. C. I believe that during the time we were living in Las Vegas, my mother had been resourceful in staying in touch with him. That is without telling him our whereabouts. After all, she had kidnapped us, but she wanted to assure him that her children were safe. I believe that she knew full well that she was putting herself at risk by returning to Michigan. She could be turned in to the authorities and arrested for kidnapping.

I was causing a big problem with my mother's plan of discreetly dropping us off without her being seen or noticed by anyone. My mother kept pleading with me that if I would just go inside this nice house, there would be a furry little bunny waiting to see me. My mom, my siblings, and I were causing a lot of commotion on the sidewalk directly in front of his house. This commotion caused the director, Mr. C, to open his door and turn the porch light on to investigate what was going on. He immediately recognized my mother and all three of us kids. This escalated the situation, and both he and my mom started raising their voices with each other. I was already frightened, but I became even more upset because of their shouting. Afraid, I started wandering down the sidewalk to get away. I wandered so far down the street that I became lost. A short while after, I looked up, and I saw a man standing over me with kind eyes and strawberry blond hair. It was Mr. C. He knelt beside me and asked, "Are you lost, little girl?" I vividly remember that I immediately trusted his warm and kind face. I took his hand, and he walked me back to his house. Momma Joy was gone. I never saw my Momma Joy again after that night on Christmas Eve.

I do know that, over the course of my mother's lifetime, she had several lovers, and she was married at least three or four times. I have been told over the years that I also have two more sisters and a brother whom I have never met. I have not been able to find them.

Mr. C made all the arrangements for placement for my siblings and myself. I was assigned back to the same foster home I was originally with, the McWilliams family. My siblings also went back to the original foster family that they had lived with. I believe with all my heart that my mother's decision to let go of her children was out of her genuine love for us. My mother knew she was not able to take care of us. I believe Mr. C knew this, too. I learned later that he cared deeply about my mother despite all of her problems, choices, and actions. I was grateful to hear later in life that Mr. C did not file charges against my mother. He had persuaded her to voluntarily sign a statement agreeing to give up custody, and her doing so would avoid any charges. And so, my mother gave up custody. Sadly, I also have no idea whatever happened to my Daddy Bob.

I settled in quickly with my foster family. A few months passed by, and it was almost Easter. My foster mother was looking forward to taking me shopping for my special Easter outfit that I would wear for church. The Easter photographs of me are very precious. I have a beautiful yellow dress, an Easter bonnet, and a pair of little white gloves. My foster family seemed so caring and proud of me.

My foster parents also had their own natural-born children. One girl and one boy, and my foster mother was pregnant with a baby boy at the time that they took me in. I have other photos from the days that we attended church, and in all of them, I am all dressed up. I know that I had a white rabbit fur muff, which I absolutely loved, that I stuffed my little hands in. I was told that I affectionately called the muff "my kitty." Also, during this time, the McWilliams had another foster child they were caring for, Mary, who was also four years old. We became fast friends, and together, we got into a lot of mischief. At some point, Mary was either adopted by another family or went back to live with her biological family. I really do not know.

The McWilliams were very good to me, and I will always be eternally grateful for that. They were sadly disappointed that they had been denied adoption. Regardless, though, for the time that I was with them, it was good. They saw me as their very own little princess, but soon, an interested adoptive family came along and expressed their intentions to adopt me.

The prospective adoptive family were the Hendersons. They started stopping by my foster family, the McWilliams, regularly after church. On one Sunday, I heard some whispering in the kitchen. I believe that I had developed a "sixth sense" early on in my life that alerts me whenever things seem awry. I felt it then, and I feel it now when something feels like it is not quite right. I had been uprooted so many times and suffered through many of my mother's bipolar episodes that I developed what I call a "danger radar." I am always on high alert. When my foster mother Sara walked out of the kitchen towards me, I immediately asked her if I was getting a new mother. She had an absolute look of shock on her face. She said, even years later, that she always wondered how I could have possibly known because they were whispering. She said I couldn't possibly have heard them. So how did I know?

The Hendersons had three boys: Jake, Bill, and Andy. One day, the Hendersons picked me up to take me tobogganing. Up to this time, I had truly little experience with snow. So far, for the vast part of my first four years of life, I have been living in the desert. The desert was sand, and this was snow. So, snow was all pretty new to me.

At the very top of a hill, I was put into a toboggan all by myself and then pushed off to ride it down the hill. I was terrified. The toboggan was racing fast down the hill, and it was bouncing wildly when suddenly the toboggan tipped over. I landed face-down in a huge pile of cold, wet snow. I was so scared at what had just happened to me that I burst into tears. This new adventure had truly scared me. But the reaction and response from Janet, my soon-to-be adoptive mother, was not at all what I expected. Her reaction to my plight was without any concern or compassion for what had just happened to me. She was completely disgusted with me and my crybaby tears and emotions. In my memories over the years of growing up and living with her, this lack of compassion held true for everything. I truly do not remember her ever showing me any compassion. So, to say that I was surprised when the Hendersons proceeded to follow through with the process to adopt me and raise me as their daughter, well, that would be an understatement.

My adoptive father, Michael, was an important Cadillac executive, but Janet ran the house. On our day in court for the final adoption proceedings, I was tired, confused, and scared, and I wanted to lay my head on Janet's shoulder for some comfort. After all, I was about to be adopted into this family as a new family member. I was going to be their daughter. I was shocked when Janet, my about-to-be new mother, pushed my head away. And this was the way it was always going to be for me with her. I learned from that day forward that I should always keep myself small and insignificant. All throughout my childhood, my adoptive mother was quick to belittle me. She would tell me that my smile was too big, or if I cried, she would tell me to turn the waterworks off. And so, I learned to not show my emotions and to try my best to stay out of her focus.

The Henderson boys were very rough on me. And it was perfectly okay with my new mother for them to push me around. In fact, she encouraged it. When she was mad at me, she would dress me up like a boy for punishment. Sometimes, I had to go to school dressed like a boy. She always diminished me. She made me feel less about myself, insecure, undeserving, and unworthy. One time, she looked me in the face, and she said to me, "I want you to know that I was going to adopt Sally. She was so beautiful; she was a whole lot prettier than you." So, obviously, her words deeply hurt me, and they stuck to me like glue. I never felt like I was a pretty girl. And Janet truly enjoyed letting those boys be mean and hurtful to me. Why did they even want to adopt me? Honestly, that is something I never figured out.

By the time I was about nine or ten years old, my adoptive parents had taken in a new foster child, a girl, and she was about fifteen years old. Her name was Kit. Together, we had to share a bedroom. Kit was a typical teenager, trying to fit in with kids her age at school, and she liked to wear a lot of makeup. One day, she asked me if I would like to wear some of her makeup. I jumped at the chance and said yes. I was really excited about the idea of wearing makeup and how it was going to make me look. I thought this would be my chance to be pretty. Especially since Janet had told me that I wasn't.

My adoptive mother, Janet, came into the bedroom to check up on us, and when she saw me with makeup on my face, she went completely berserk on poor Kit. She started yelling at the top of her lungs, and she called Kit a tramp. What a terrible day this was. I felt so bad for poor Kit. Soon after this day, Kit was sent back to the orphanage. I was shocked, afraid, and confused. I did not understand. I wondered what possibly was so terribly wrong about putting on some make-up. Why was Kit called a tramp and then sent back to the orphanage? It was just makeup. It could be washed off. There was no permanent harm.

Cleaning the house for my adoptive parents, especially washing down all the walls, was a really a big deal. One day, when I was doing my assigned cleaning duties, I happened to find a box of photos. Obviously, I was curious, so I started looking through them. Some of the photos that I was looking at showed the Hendersons camping out, and they were together with other men and women. I'm not really sure what I was looking at, but whatever it was, when Janet, my adoptive mom, came into the room, she went absolutely berserk on me. I am not sure, but there must have been some secrets in that box of photos that she didn't want anyone to know about.

My life living there always seemed like I could never do anything right. Janet thought that my smile was too big, that I didn't turn the water faucet off right, and I couldn't even cry right. So, I always felt that I was unattractive, stupid, and a terrible person, that I was worthless, and nobody loved me or wanted me. Her encouraging her boys to be rough and mean to me reinforced my thinking that I had no real worth. Nobody cared or wanted me. I believe she resented me. So again, I wondered and still ask myself, to this day, why did she even take me in? Why did they adopt me?

It was so hurtful to me that every year, for summer vacation, my adoptive parents took their boys on vacation, but they never took me. I was always sent to the grandparents' house, who were Janet's parents. The message that I felt she was sending to me was that I was not truly part of their family. I was just a child they adopted, and I was not as important to them as their own natural-born children.

But thank goodness for those grandparents. They were special and good to me. I do fondly remember eating sardines with my adoptive grandfather. I felt close to him, and together we had a special bond. In 1967, the year of the riots in Detroit, Grandma and Grandpa, Janet's parents, and her brother, Uncle Joe, decided it was time to move out of the city. Together, they moved to a small town that was on a lake. I loved the special time that we had at the lake. We did water skiing, fishing, and ice skating in the winter. It was like every day was a vacation.

At about the age of fourteen, I started feeling surer of myself. One day, when the whole family was out at the lake, one of my adoptive brothers was being mean to me out on the boat dock. He was shoving and pushing me. Well, that day, I decided that I had taken his and his brother's meanness long enough. So, without any hesitation, I picked up a hand full of sand, and I grounded that sand right into his face. I was burning hot mad. This was not so good for me. Janet was up on the shore by the house, and she happened to see everything, and she was livid. I knew that this was not going to turn out well for me. I knew it was not going to matter what her son had done to me. She banished me from their house. I was kicked out. She sent me away to live at her sister's house. This move to her sister's house turned out not to be a very good move for me at all. While I was living with her sister, I think I was shocked and deeply hurt by how I was treated, and because of that, I started acting out. I started smoking and doing a lot of other things that I shouldn't have been doing.

At some point, a long time after, I was allowed to move back to my adoptive parents' house. By this time, I had blossomed and grown up more. In my opinion, I believe that I was pretty. I am not sure what Janet thought. I had earned some babysitting money, so I was able to buy myself some pretty clothes. Michael, my adoptive father, noticed how I had matured and that I was attractive. It turned out that he really liked what he was seeing. One day, while at the house, he discreetly slipped me a note that said, "If you ever have a thought or any feelings about having sex with your father, I want you to know it is completely normal." He then told me to throw the note in the fireplace so that no one would know. That note totally shocked me, and it scared me to death. It took my breath away. From that day forward, I felt very uneasy living there. About a month later, because I no longer felt safe, I ran away from home. I was fifteen years old.

I was naïve and underage. Because I was a runaway, per the law, when caught, I would be sent to a juvenile home. That was unless there was a family member on Michael's side who would take me in. A family member of my adoptive father did end up taking me in. It was Michael's nephew and his wife. Unhappy living there, I left at the age of sixteen.

Later, when I was on my own, at about age seventeen, I subleased an apartment across from a courthouse. I attended a Lutheran church close by. At this church, I found that the parishioners could be cold and indifferent. They did not seem as warm and caring as you would hope church people would normally be. But I was thirsty for religion, and I wanted to learn more about God. I started reading the Bible. The church pastor had a son named Jimmy, and someone decided that it would be good to introduce me to him. For both of us, it felt like we were meant to be together, and we fell instantly in love. We meshed well together, and we enjoyed spending as much time together as possible.

This was a happy time in my life. I got along well with both of his parents. I have fond memories of spending a wonderful and lazy summer with Jimmy. I was in love, and he loved me. He always wanted me around. It was not a smart decision, but I decided to quit high school. I only had one more class that I needed to graduate. So, truly, it was not smart at all on my part to quit school. I was working at the time, so going to school just did not seem important to me. Jimmy and my job were all that I cared about. I felt that was all I needed.

Fortunately, for my sake, the pastor's wife was a school counselor, so together, she and her husband got me back on track so that I could graduate. I am most thankful that they were watching out for me.

There was a chiropractor who I knew because he attended the same Lutheran church. He was a good Christian man, and he had hired me to work in the office at his practice. Knowing and working for him was important and significant in my life. One day, when I was doing some office filing, I saw the name of my foster family in one of the file folders. Obviously, they were patients there. A few months later, they walked into the office for an appointment with the doctor. All it took for me was one look, and I immediately recognized them. But I was not sure how to start a conversation, so finally, I asked them if they had ever taken foster kids in. Sara McWilliams smiled and replied, "Yes, we did, and I would recognize you anywhere." I immediately felt a special vibe. This was at a time in my life when it was hard for me to trust anyone. My boyfriend was away in Oklahoma, going to divinity college and studying to be a pastor. I missed him and his love and support.

Soon after this encounter at the office, a girl that I knew from school called and said she had a one-way plane ticket for me. She wanted me to fly out to Boston and live with her. I was seventeen years old. I decided that I would take the leap. Soon after I arrived there, I got a job at a jeans store. During this entire time, my foster family stayed in touch with me. At Christmas time, I flew back to see Jimmy, who would be home on break from school. My foster family called and invited me to come over for a visit. I accepted the invitation, and we ended up staying up all through the night talking about our lives. One might wonder why did I stay connected with my foster family? I think it is about feeling like you belong somewhere and you are part of something. To feel like someone genuinely cares about you. The McWilliams, my foster family, provided me with that. My adoptive family never did.

After the holiday was over, I went back to Boston, and several months later, my foster family sent me a one-way plane ticket. I was going through some depression, so I felt that it would be good for me to go back. At that time, they wanted me to consider adult adoption. Adult adoption occurs when a former foster child who was not legally available for adoption at the time they were living with them grows close to their foster family and wants to be adopted. At this time in my life, this was a really big "no" for me. But without any hesitation in saying this, I know that my life growing up would have been so much better with them as my adoptive parents.

Janet, my adoptive mother, was always such a backbiter, and I knew she could not be trusted. I would hear her all the time, talking behind my back about me, sniping about me. One time, while we were out at the lake, the conversations about me that I overheard echoed clearly. You know how it is with voices carrying over the water. I could hear her saying that I was stocky, and she said a lot of other mean and hurtful things. But to my face, when I was standing in front of her, she always had a smile on. She was a mean and hateful person, for sure. Maybe she was insecure about herself.

Sadly, my sweetheart Jimmy and I broke up. I truly loved him, and our breakup was hard for me. My foster dad wanted to reconnect me with my biological siblings. He thought this would be good for me at this time in my life. He knew that Mr. C from the adoption agency knew how to locate them. Mr. C followed through and made the arrangements for myself and my siblings to meet.

My poor sister had not fared that well. She had suffered sexual abuse in foster care and at the orphanage. But even so, she was still a powerhouse of a person. She married a guy not out of love but to escape the abuse. She falsified her legal documents to be of the legal age to marry. Next, I met my brother Max, and I thought he was a genius. I ended up becoming close with both of my siblings.

My sister knew where our half-brothers and sisters were. They also wanted to meet, and so did my biological father. It was all arranged, and I met my real dad, Roger. He was good-looking, just as I had been told he was. I felt bad, though, that my dad rejected and ignored my sister, and he fawned all over me. At some point, he convinced me to come and live with him in Wisconsin. This felt like another one of those moments in time when I believed that this was a meant-to-be for me. After all, this was my real father, and he wanted me to live with him. His offer was a way out of a situation that I was in at the time, and I felt I could truly better my life. So, I made that move to Wisconsin to live with my dad.

It ended up that my dad was a barfly and a womanizer. He used women, and he didn't respect them. He would live with them and then live off of them. I really did not like who my father was at all. So, I started going back and forth between Michigan and Wisconsin. During that time, I ended up meeting a guy named Dan, who had two kids. Dan and I became involved, and I ended up getting pregnant. That relationship truly did not end well. Dan did not want another child. He was not at all happy that I was pregnant. In fact, he started accusing me of sleeping with other men and denying that this could even possibly be his child, that that was the farthest thing from the truth, and that this definitely was not his child. But I had not been involved with anyone else. I was nineteen years old, scared, and not sure of what to do, and so, once again, I packed my belongings to move and make my way back to my foster family.

Being pregnant with my first child felt extremely special and important to me. I wanted to be the best mother possible. That is, if I was even going to keep the baby. I was having thoughts that this baby might be better off with an adoptive family. I wanted to be sure about my decision. My first step was to improve myself, so I started taking college classes to become that better self. I had a lot to think about and figure out.

My foster mother, Sara, sent me to live with her oldest daughter, Liz. At the time, she was married to a guy who could not keep a job because he always rubbed people the wrong way. I was eight months pregnant. A month went by, now I was nine months pregnant, and she decided to put her house up for sale. The realtor selling her house happened to meet me and told Liz that he was interested in me. I thought he had to be a complete lunatic. But Liz convinced me there was no harm in going to dinner with the guy. I still don't get it. I am nineteen years old and nine months pregnant. She explained to me that some men are enamored with pregnant women. I guess so, because he lost interest in me after the baby was born and I was no longer pregnant.

My college classes were not yet over when my son Joey was born. My foster family, the McWilliams, once again stepped in and offered to help by watching him throughout the week while I finished up my classes. My classes would be over in February.

So, over Christmas break, I was invited to the McWilliams Christmas celebration. Their tradition was to attend church on Christmas Eve, then meet afterward for some family time. That year, it was the McWilliams' son, Derek, and his wife Denise's turn to host the event. I went to church with them and met for the first time, Denise's brother, Brad. I had my son, Joey, with me, and Brad seemed to take quite an interest in him. Of course, that got my attention! A few weeks later, Brad's sister called me, told me that her brother Brad wanted to go out with me, and asked if I would be amenable to going on a double date with her and Derek. I responded by telling her that I would like Brad to call me himself. He did, and we all went to the movies for our first date...and so, it began.

Soon, Brad and I were an item. Things between us progressed, and one day, he asked me to marry him, and I said yes. I had just completed my program at school and had started a new job, so I thought our wedding date would not be until sometime later. But between his family and my foster family's bidding, we set a date that was only a few months after our engagement.

Shortly after we were married, Brad asked me if he could adopt my son. After some discussion (I wanted to make sure he was firmly set to take on the emotional responsibility of such a decision after everything that I had been through), and once I was convinced, I agreed. It felt right. We petitioned the court and followed through with the adoption.

A couple of years later, Brad and I had a baby girl. We remained together and married for twenty-three years. But we could not hold it together any longer and divorced. Both children were affected by the divorce because of the reasons that our marriage fell apart and because we couldn't make it work. They were adults at the time, and we tried to keep things civil during and after the divorce, even taking turns hosting the holiday gatherings.

I moved on after our divorce and was blessed to have someone new come into my life. We are married, and I consider him to be my best friend. While my children have not fully embraced him, he thinks of them as his own. He never had children of his own. It has been a long trek for all of us, but little by little, a relationship has formed.

I have contemplated all the help that I received along the way over the years. When I find myself in a situation where I see someone who needs help, I immediately reach out and offer to help them. I have taken in ladies who were in my circle of friends and who were going through abusive marriages, and their children were at risk. There are a lot of stories that, in retrospect, I strongly feel that I am paying things forward, so to speak.

As time passes on, I reflect on all the times when I was at risk to danger, and I can clearly see that God's hand was on my life, and He was watching over me. I often say that God pays attention to orphans and widows.

I had some trouble with both of my children that affected our relationship. I was always the one to demonstrate "tough love" so that they would learn from the consequences. It often broke my heart to do so. But as adults, we have reconciled with our past.

After a bout with stomach cancer, following a very difficult financial season in my life, I started thinking about my mortality. I realized I had been a wife, mother, and professional careerist, but I had never really done anything just for me. Thinking back, I targeted that when I was in high school; I was pretty good at pen and ink drawings. So, one day, I purchased some art supplies and started painting. Six years later, I am painting artwork that some folks even want to buy! Art has been a tremendous therapy for me. One of the series that I have painted is an "old boat series." It takes me back in time to spending early mornings with my grandfather from my adoptive family, the Hendersons, and being out on the lake, fishing. I also have a strong feeling that being on the water must be in my DNA, given that my biological father was a merchant marine. I am deeply inspired by the handiwork of God in my landscape paintings as well.

Just this year, the last of my biological siblings passed away, and I am now the only one left. I have a close relationship with my sister's daughter, my niece, and we often talk about her mother's effect on our lives. While I am sad that both my siblings are gone, I am happy that I was afforded the opportunity to build a relationship with them, even though it was later in life. Again, I feel the hand of God in all that has happened to me, and I am grateful.

When you have suffered emotional abuse, you are vigilant; you always look for the other shoe to drop. You see things because you have lived a life where, at any moment, something could happen, something that could change everything, and your life could be in danger. My radar for spotting a bad situation is highly sensitive. I can walk into a room, scope it out, and see the danger and the "beware" signs that are in the room.

My husband is most proud of me that I am stepping forward to share and tell my story. He feels that bringing up my painful past will help others. We both feel that being open and honest about your own life opens the door for others to be brave and have the courage to share their pain and help with their healing.

That is my prayer, and that is also my sincere hope.

CHAPTER ELEVEN:

I WANTED TO BE AWESOME, STRIKING, AND BODACIOUS

ISABELLA'S INTERVIEW AND STORY.

I was born in 1986 in New York City, the Big Apple, as they call it. My mom says life back then, in the eighties, was really hopping. Pop culture was emerging, which showcased some brand-new trends and helped to kick off a new kind of vibe and energy that surrounded us. MTV and cable TV were just coming out, and for sure, I was right smack in front of our television as soon as I was old enough to take it all in. I watched and studied all of it. The trendy new hairstyles, the way they dressed, the music, the movies, and the lifestyles. I grew up in what I thought were some amazing times, and I wanted to be just like the stars that I was watching on MTV. I wanted to be awesome, striking, and bodacious.

I feel that I had what one would consider a fairly *normal* childhood. I think our family was pretty much that typical Italian family. Whenever you walked into our house, you immediately caught the aroma of garlic and my mother's special spaghetti sauce that was simmering on the stove in the kitchen. We always had a lot of relatives coming and going. We had discipline when we needed it, but we had a lot of love, too. My dad treated me like a little princess. My mom was very warm and loving. I had an older sister, a younger sister, and a brother.

In high school, I met a guy named Angelo. I instantly fell in love with him. I had been preparing for this time in my life by studying how celebrities and trendsetters lived, and I had big plans for my life. Thinking that I had all the answers for my future, I dropped out of school at the age of sixteen and enrolled in beauty school. I graduated from beauty school when I was eighteen years old. I loved that I had made this my career choice, and I was focused on becoming a highly recommended professional stylist. Still, today, I love what I do, and I believe that I am very good at it. I have a large client following and I am currently working in an upscale and exclusive salon in southern Florida.

I was still in love with my high school sweetheart, Angelo, and so, at age twenty-one, we decided that we wanted to get married. Soon after, we took our vows, and we were blessed with a beautiful and healthy baby boy. We both felt that we had it all. We would be living the best possible life with grand expectations for a whole lot more to come. But sadly, that was not our luck. So many problems and worries began to happen for us.

These were not little problems that we were facing either. We had to confront some life-threatening, live-or-die problems. I had a C-section for the birth of our son, and I suffered some major complications from it. I was kept confined to the hospital for over a month, with doctors trying to figure out what was wrong with me. For over a month, I lay in that hospital bed, scared to death that I was surely dying. I couldn't stop crying and thinking about my beautiful baby boy Max. If I died, he would have to grow up without his mother and all the love and affection that I would have surrounded him with. I thought this was all so unfair, and why was this happening to me, my husband Angelo, and our son? I should have been home, in my baby's nursery, fussing over him, cuddling him, and loving him. I should have been welcoming our friends and family to our home to meet and hold our new son. We were losing all hope after a month had gone by. Then, finally, they found the cause. During the C-section for my delivery, the doctor punctured my artery. I was bleeding to death. I had been given so many transfusions just to keep me alive. I was extremely weak and still terrified, knowing that I was so close to death and leaving this world and everyone that I loved. It was such a terrifying time, and it was heartbreaking not being able to bond with my baby. My heart ached at the thought of him needing his mother, and I was not there for him.

It was just six months later that my husband Angelo started waking up at night crying and moaning, saying that he did not feel well. This went on for a while, and I was waking up to take care of the baby and Angelo. Another crisis was upon us when Angelo was diagnosed with suffering from kidney failure. We were told that he desperately needed a kidney transplant or he would die. Angelo had to begin dialysis treatments right away. So, here we are facing another life-threatening crisis. Angelo was so sick that I had no choice; I had to go to work full-time to be able to pay our bills and support us. Even though I was working full time, I still needed to continue to help take care of my sick husband while also caring for our son. This was a strain on all of us and a very scary and depressing time. A time when you start questioning the *why* for all of this and *why* it was happening to us. When our son Max was about two years old, my husband Angelo's brother gave Angelo one of his kidneys to save his life. The transplant, thankfully, was successful. But by this time, I was so unhappy and disillusioned about everything. It was extremely hard managing it all. Everything we had been through had put a terrible strain on our marriage. I think we had just grown apart because our entire marriage had been one crisis after another.

When our son Max was about three years old, tragedy struck again. My brother, who I always admired and adored, had served for five years in the military. He was stationed in Iraq. When he returned home, he truly never seemed to be the same brother and that special guy that I knew and loved. He had changed into someone I did not really know anymore. He was drinking heavily, and he was also taking Xanax, using cocaine, and using heroin. He was in a bad place, and he was desperately trying to block out the nightmares from Iraq and even block out the life that he had been living since he had returned home. He was in so much pain; you could see it in his sad eyes. Not like the pain you would have from a broken bone or a bad back. He had a sad, unhappy, dark look. A look that said, "I am in a dark and unhappy place in my life." He was struggling to take part in anything good that he could have been doing to try and make things better for himself. He was suffering from PTSD, and it was heartbreaking to see him this way. Before his time serving in Iraq, he was a warm, intelligent, and fun-loving guy. Now, that guy, it seemed, was lost forever.

He did have a girlfriend that he started seeing. Before they started dating, she had been his best friend's girlfriend. I felt that my brother really seemed to care about this girl, and while they were dating, she became pregnant. My brother was sincerely happy about having a baby, which was a light of hope, knowing that he had found some happiness. He told her that he loved her, and that he wanted to marry her and have their baby. My brother marrying her and having that baby seemed to be the one thing that he could feel good about. But unfortunately, she felt very differently about all of it. She did not want to marry him, and she also did not want to have his baby. She had an abortion, and that was the tipping point and the downfall for my brother. Soon after, he was found dead in his room, and drugs were found.

When my brother died, my entire world crumbled, too. I completely fell apart. It seemed like all of it was just too much. I thought it was so unfair that all of this was happening to us. I kept asking myself why. I wasn't prepared to know how to handle all these tragedies and sadness, and now my brother's suicide.

I had not been happy for an exceptionally long time in my marriage, so I told Angelo that I was filing for a divorce. We were separated for about a year when I started dating another guy named Bruno. Bruno came from a wealthy family, and he lived the fast life with his money and his big connections. He was everything that I saw as living life large and being exciting. He had the money and the influence, and he commanded respect. I was experiencing a rich lifestyle that I had never had before. I felt like I was someone special because he made me feel that way. I loved the lavish lifestyle. He showered me with expensive jewelry, designer clothes, and a luxury car. We ate at expensive restaurants, we traveled all over, and all I ever had to do was simply ask for whatever it was that I wanted.

I am riding high, we are enjoying life in a big way, and then I find out that I am pregnant. Bruno and I decided to get married, and I gave birth to a baby boy that we named Gino. My first son, Max, had just turned four years old. I was incredibly happy that I had been blessed with two beautiful boys.

Soon after Gino was born, it was discovered that my baby boy, Gino, was not a healthy baby. He was suffering from extremely high fevers, which then brought on seizures. The doctors and specialists were struggling to find out what was causing this. The fevers and seizures Gino suffered continued for the first three years of his fragile life. During that time, he was in and out of the hospital. I have always highly suspected that his dad was using drugs when I became pregnant, which might have affected our son. Gino was also asthmatic, and he had several bouts of pneumonia. Because Gino was so sickly and in and out of the hospital, I had to rely on my ex-husband to take care of our son Max. It was the best thing for poor little Max because Gino consumed all my time and energy.

During this span of time of hospitals, doctors, and caring for Gino, my husband, Bruno, Gino's father, for the most part, was never around. Bruno's fast lifestyle that he wanted to live did not include a sick baby and an exhausted and concerned mother. He was a high-rolling gambler, a partier, and a big spender. He had places to be and people to see, and caring for a sick child and his wife was not part of his concern or on his agenda. Soon, he became not only neglectful but also mean, and we were having arguments that became physical. He was physically hurting and abusing me. I was terrified of him, and I was even more afraid because I was so vulnerable and weak because I was exhausted from worrying and caring for our son. I was without any support, help, or places to turn to. I was giving all my energy and time to our very sick son. Sometimes, Bruno would take the keys to the car so that I could not leave; he would be gone for days, and many times, there was not much food in the house. We were not poor. Not poor at all. We had lots of beautiful furnishings and things. But providing the very basics for his wife and son was not important to him at this point. He did not sign up for this, and he did not care about what happened to either of us. He was using drugs, so his priorities did not include his family. I knew I could no longer exist living in this situation, and my mind was racing with thoughts of just giving up. I felt like my life was simply not worth living anymore. I was feeling hopeless.

The plan that I decided to put into place was secretly sneaking away and taking our son to my sister's house. Once there, I planned to leave my son Gino with her. I felt confident that my baby boy would be safe there and well cared for. At this point in my life, I felt that everyone would be better off without me. I was considering suicide. This was a very desperate time in my life, and I just did not care anymore. I just wanted the pain to stop, and I was so tired of it all. My brother flashed in and out of my thoughts, and I sensed that I knew what he might have felt like.

One night, when Bruno was home and he had passed out, I found the keys to my car, which he had hidden. I grabbed a few things to pack for myself and Gino, and we made our escape. We were running away from home. My precious baby boy and I were running away from the monster that we lived with.

We made it to my sister's house, which was in another state. When I arrived at her house, I was an absolute emotional mess. I said my goodbyes to little Gino and my sister, and I left. But my plan to take my life was not meant to be. Every time I thought about how and when I would do it, I would see my little boy's sweet face looking up at me. I ached deep down inside myself, knowing with every fiber within me that this little boy needed his mother, and so did my son Max. I did not want to miss seeing my boys growing up.

I finally found a women's shelter that helped me. This place of refuge absolutely saved my life. It made an enormous difference in my desperate situation. Their refuge provided me with safety and support. Their counseling gave me hope and helped me to begin my journey back to get my life on a better path. I started praying, and I began believing in God and having faith in that "this too shall pass." When you find yourself in the deepest depths of darkness on earth, without any hope, and not caring about living another day, having God to turn to in prayer gives you a reason to have enough faith to go on.

I was able to eventually divorce Bruno. But dealing with the court system and their enforcing visitations proved to be, over and over again, that it was not going to be easy for my son or for me. Many times, Gino would return home after visiting his father's house with tales of bizarre episodes with friends and girl-friends. Drugs, sex, alcohol, and even animal abuse.

Bruno also worked the court system by not paying child sup-port, and then, when going to court, he would provide false doc-uments for his income to keep the payments so low that I could not even afford a lot of the basics. I was working as a hairdresser, but I was not making enough to afford the care needed for two boys, schooling, and, along with that, our housing, too. On top of that, I needed an attorney each time we went to court. I could not afford one, and, somehow, financially, I did not qualify for legal aid. My ex-husband, on the other hand, could afford a top attor-ney. So, I was at a disadvantage in court at every turn.

Bruno's girlfriend was always trying to pick a fight with me over anything and everything. I do not know if it was jealousy or she was and just is a mean and crazy woman. But on one bizarre occasion, she actually punched herself in the eye and in her face. When I arrived at the house to pick up my son, she called the police and had me arrested for assault. She told the police that I had attacked her. I spent that night in jail. Unfortunately, because of that, I have an assault charge against me, and it is on my permanent record for something that I absolutely did not do. It is beyond my understanding how the bad guys seem to always have the advantage. Money talks, and people with power know how to work the system. They are street-smart, which I am not. I have never even dreamed of faking or falsifying something to intentionally get someone arrested.

After years of this craziness, along came into my life someone special who genuinely cares about me and my situation, and he stepped in to help me. Soon, because of him and his kind heart, I had an attorney to help me win against my ex-husband in court. Soon, he was helping me get back on track with my finances and helping with my needs for myself and my children. Some may call this person my sugar daddy because there is an age difference. But I am not about using labels for people. To me, he is my guardian angel and the man that I have grown to love over time. He is someone who rescued me from some extremely hard, dark, and desperate times because he cared. He cared not just about me but also about my children.

He came into my life shortly after a past boyfriend whom I still cared about died suddenly. It was determined that he died from an overdose. Perhaps our coming together was heaven-sent so that he could help me through some very hard times. For where I am now, he may want to mean more to me or have more of me in his life. We are taking it day by day and focusing on all the good that we have now in our lives.

I genuinely enjoy spending time with my boys and watching them grow up. I remember well that there was one point in my life when I thought my life was not worth living. I get cold chills whenever I think back to that time because I was remarkably close to ending it all. This relatively calmer climate in my life is working. The anxiety and panic are manageable. I know I am not in control of everything. I believe that God is in control, and what is different in my life now is that I pray, and I listen. I never want to go back to those dark places.

I am working on building a better foundation that includes praying, having faith, yoga, positive energy and thinking, and doing things that make us happy. I love the ocean, the sunshine that warms my face and warms my soul. I need healing. I need recovery, and I need restoration.

I know what it feels like to be without hope and not wanting to live. I remember my brother who took his life and the sadness and desperation he felt. I know what it feels like to be scared and fear for my life. I know what pain feels like and what evil looks like. For now, what I need most is some rest and healing, to love my boys, and to work on whatever it is that helps to make this life better.

There are many things I have gotten wrong in the choices that I have made thus far in my life. And I am just thirty-eight years old. So, if I can offer help or insight to others, I would say be happy about all the good things, no matter how small. And sometimes, when you choose the high roller, the fast Eddie, looking for excitement and more out of life, it might be one of the biggest mistakes that you make. Think about the what-ifs. Listen to your inner self and your intuition and turn down the sound to the loud pounding bass that rings in your ears, telling you the wilder side is more exciting, that it is a good choice, and that it will be more fun. Making that choice might possibly be your worst choice of all. It might cause you to think it is all hopeless.

Remembering my days of sitting in front of the TV when I was a young girl, I wanted to be awesome, striking, and bodacious. Well, I had a taste of that.

Now, what I want is happiness, security, love, faith, and hope for a better life and future for myself and my family.

I hope for the very same for others.

Chapter Twelve:

You Can't Keep Me Down No Matter How Hard You Try

MAX'S INTERVIEW AND STORY.

The day I was released from prison, I walked out of there barefoot. I didn't have a pair of shoes, a place to go, or a car to drive, and I had very little money. I had just served a ten-year sentence for a crime that did not really happen. You might be thinking, *Oh yeah, I have heard that before*. But when you are poor and cannot afford to have good legal help, many times, for a lot of people, you are locked up. I do not feel that I was important enough for the powers that be to dig deep into the evidence to find out the truth. I was disposable, I was a nobody. I was not an important, well-connected person who could pull or expect favors within the system. I was just a poor country boy who had suffered a hard life growing up, and I was still trying to figure things out.

The story that I want to share is not about the unfairness and the broken system, how I suffered, and how I was sentenced to prison because of it. I don't want to waste my breath or the words on paper and in this chapter to try and explain what happened. It just did. It's not like my retelling of that whole story, twenty-seven years later, is going to change anything.

There are plenty of people who say they are innocent when they are not. There are also many others who are innocent and who are locked up for years, sometimes for their entire life. We hear about those people on the news. Stories such as those from the Innocence Project and other non-profits like them that help to exonerate wrongly accused. But for me, I am labeled; I have a record. One that I am stuck with for the rest of my life.

My record states that I am a convicted felon. I feel a lump coming up in my throat, and I start to cry and choke when I think about it or say it out loud. Because I know my conviction was unjust and unfair. So, having to live with this, which affects so much in my life, I can at least take comfort in knowing that God knows the truth. It does not matter about anyone else. God is my vindicator, my strength, and the reason that my life is good now. I am happily married, and I have a close, loving relationship with my family. When I lay down to sleep at night, I feel good about the person that I am and good about my strong faith in God. I rest and sleep better now than I ever did before. My faith is my protector. You hear people say that when you hit rock bottom, and you have lost all hope, there is one thing that saved them. Time and time again, it is because of their belief that there is a God, and simply said, "He will help you." A person who is living their life without hope is in such a dark, lonely, and awful place.

I referred to myself as a country boy who had a hard life. To elaborate on that, I know without the slightest doubt that my life was a living nightmare. It started at the young age of five, with suffering abuse in several different foster care homes. I was in foster care because my mother was incarcerated. After she was released from prison, she remarried, and she was able to get myself and my four siblings back. But in comparison, the abuse that I suffered in foster care, which I thought was bad, did not even begin to compare to the sexual, physical, and emotional abuse I suffered at the hands of my stepfather. From the age of six until the age of seventeen, the daily abuse in our house is beyond what I could explain and describe. I should be dead. I do not know how I survived. The day that I left home for good and joined the U.S. Marine Corps was the escape plan that I had been begging and waiting for. I was desperate to escape the nightmare that myself, my siblings, and my mother had been suffering. I could not protect them, and I could not protect myself.

There were many times, growing up, that I felt for sure that my stepfather had tried to kill me. And there were just as many times that I truly wished he had because many times I wanted to die. I did not want to suffer any longer. I constantly wished that he were dead. I wished all kinds of terrible diseases, accidents, and others on him just to stop the pain we were all suffering. He truly was the devil himself, beating all of us until we were limp and had lost the will to live or to fight back. We were all so desperate, begging for someone to help us. But no one could. There were many dark days and times when I wanted to give up. But for whatever reason, I didn't. I believe with all my heart that it was God who spared my life. But during this time in my life, I really did not know God and the teachings about God. But I cannot give any other explanation of why I did not die at the hands of my stepfather. The beatings were that bad. The life-threatening things he did to me were that bad.

One time, I was trying to light a hot water heater, and it had a flame flashback, which severely burnt both of my eyes. My mother and stepfather took me to the hospital. I was treated, and after being treated, I left that day with eye patches that completely covered both of my eyes. The hospital doctor told us that he was not sure that I would ever regain my sight. There was a strong possibility that I would be blind. When we returned home, my stepfather dropped my mother back off at the truck stop restaurant that they owned so that she could get back to work and cooking. My stepfather then took me to the house, which was a little bit further back on our property from the restaurant. As soon as we got inside of the house, he led me straight to the basement stairs. He guided me down two of the steps, and then he shoved me. I fell to the bottom of the staircase, which was about fifteen steps to the bottom and the basement floor. I was hurt badly from the fall, but I was so scared because I was in complete darkness. I was terrified. I was hurt, and I could not see. I crawled around and tried to feel my way around until I found a wall that I could lean up against. My stepfather did this to me because he was angry that he had a medical bill that he had to pay, and on top of that, now he had this blind and stupid kid who was useless. I could not do the work that he demanded and expected any longer. I do not know how many days I was left down in the basement. Because I was not able to see, I couldn't tell if it was night or day. I remember how terrified I was. I honestly thought that I was going to die down there. I thought that this time, he would get what he really wanted. He wanted me dead. My mother was forbidden to even open the basement door.

So, my time in the service as a new recruit when I went into the Marine Corps came pretty easy enough for me. That is because the harsh treatment at camp to whip us into shape did not even begin to compare to the beatings and verbal abuse that I had endured living at home. One time, a drill sergeant punched me, and I reacted and punched him back. I felt for sure either my days in the service would be over or I would be locked up and thrown in the brig. Fortunately, my memory is that because of my lack of good judgment, my punishment was what seemed like a million push-ups.

Still today, it is hard for me to see a child or a woman being mistreated. The nightmares from my past immediately resurface. It triggers all the terror and pain from my past. But I have learned to control those triggers, and now, instead of wanting to fight the abuser, I try to use my voice to call them out. I must be careful now because of my criminal record. I cannot risk being arrested for a felony on my record. But I also can't let a helpless woman or child be beaten without saying something.

I have been married five times. What I can say to make it not seem as bad as one might think, and it is true, it took me five times to find the right woman. My wife, whom I am with now, makes me a better person and a better man. I have never been happier in my life than I am now. I made a lot of mistakes before we found each other. And I know she deeply loves and cares about me. We have been married for nine years. I cannot begin to express how lucky I feel.

Even though prison was hard, and it was ten years of my life, it was also where I found God. Remember what I said about my being at the absolute bottom of the barrel and not wanting to live anymore? Well, when you are locked up, that's being at the bottom. You are locked up in a place where you think about what else can you lose. You are a prisoner in every sense of the word. This is a time in your life when you must start looking for something good to come out of all this. I needed to find a way to survive this because ten years is a long time. And so, thankfully, I did find something good to come out of all of it. For me, it was the prison ministry program. For the most part, I went to prison as a non-believer. I just did not know much about church and God. And to be honest, it was hard to believe in God. How could there be a God after the horrible life I had lived? When every day of your life you questioned if there was a God, because if there was, why were we all suffering the abuse that we did? It was very confusing. It was hard to believe a God even existed.

You often hear that rehabilitation in prisons does not work. And I would agree that not everybody who comes out of prison is rehabilitated. But there are some crucial factors to look at when someone is released from prison. Some people who are paroled have nowhere to go. They either do not have a family, or their family does not want to have anything to do with them. And so, they have little choice but to go back into doing whatever it was that caused them to go to prison to begin with.

We, as a society and government, could do better. The people in power could put a focus on this problem and maybe a little less focus on some other things. We don't want to go down that road and question all the many areas that our government invests time and money in. That is not the purpose of my sharing. I am not delving into how the government works or about politics. So, the reasons for not making what seem to be important and necessary changes in the many different areas of our country are way beyond my understanding. But I do think that, as a country, we could do a better job on critical issues and problems like this and make the prison parolee's situation a bigger priority! It is just like our veterans who fought for our country, and many are now sleeping on the streets because they are poor, sick, and homeless. Our Constitution states: "We the people, For the people,"—but what people are we talking about? Many people are simply forgotten and seem to be considered less important. And I was a proud marine and wanted to serve my country. Regardless, to this day, I remain proud.

There are a lot of tough guys in prison. The ones that you know not to cross and stay out of their way. You have heard of a wolf in sheep's clothing—a person with a pleasant and friendly appearance that hides the fact that they are evil. If you are not careful, you could fall prey to some pretty evil wolves. But I also knew and saw some tough guys, even murderers, who would break down and cry during some of the prison ministry sermons. One such tough guy was in prison for manslaughter with no chance for parole. He had killed five family members in cold blood, and he shared that he was tormented over this. He said at the time when it happened, he was high on drugs and out of his mind. Because of what he did, he hated himself, and the memories were haunting him. One day, he came by my cell as I was lying on my bunk reading. He asked me if he could talk with me, and I could see that he had tears in his eyes. This convicted killer was crying and standing outside my cell door. But it happens: tall, tough, and muscular men in tears. He asked me to help him pray and to ask for God's forgiveness. He said he needed to have God forgive him in the way that I had been telling him it was possible. We also were praying and hearing about this with the prayer teams that were part of the prison ministry. So, that day, we both knelt at my bunk, and we prayed together for God's forgiveness. When we were done praying, I told him to believe that God forgave him and that he could not go back on God's promise. I told him that once you ask for His forgiveness, it will be given. I said he should believe this to be true. This changed his life going forward. For all the remaining days that I know about while I was still serving, he never stopped believing. Some men in the prison referred to me as a Bible thumper. *Well*, I thought, *okay, you can call me whatever you want*. My prayers and my Bible got me through it all.

I am here to shout to the mountains that prison ministries are the most important help you can offer inside of a prison. My estimation of what I saw in the numbers of people who dedicated their life to God was at least 35 to 40 percent. I personally knew hundreds who attended their services and gave testimony. For myself, my testimony to share is that the years that I spent in prison saved my life, and I came out of prison a better person. For the first time in my life, because of prison ministries, I felt like I mattered. Somebody cared. That there was a God, and He would be there to answer my prayers. This God that they taught us about, He loved me, and I should have faith in Him. He would guide me, protect me, and be with me always. I read the Bible several times; I can't even begin to know how many times. The verses I read gave me hope, comfort, and the will to go on. So, for a child who grew up feeling worthless, unloved, abused, and told to be stupid, having God in my life gave me, for the first time, some meaning and purpose. I know that my mother loved me. But because she was so weak, she suffered, and her children suffered years of terrible abuse. I love my mother, who has now left this world, but my heart will always ache, remembering the pain that we all endured because of her bad choices. We all make mistakes, and I am proof of that, too. But it is what we do to make changes in our life to make things better. I try to strive hard each and every day to be better than I was the day before.

A little bit about who Kairos is and what Kairos ministries do is best understood by sharing how they got started. Before Kairos was formed, there was an existing program already in place that was called Cursillo, which is a Catholic-based training program. In 1978, six states were bringing the Cursillo program, which was a series of short ministry courses, into prisons. The national Cursillo organization reviewed their programming, and they determined that these ministries needed to be supervised by a central authority. They determined that the format needed to be modified so it would be more closely beneficial and more specific for the inmates and their needs. Nine volunteers stepped forward, who are affectionately referred to as the "Nine Old Men." These nine men redesigned and renamed the program "Kairos," which in Greek means "God's Special Time."

In 1979, the first Kairos Prison Ministry weekend began. Following that very first weekend and the resounding positive outcome, the Cursillo ministries stopped their existing programming in all the prisons and joined the Kairos Prison Ministry. The Kairos program is called Kairos Inside. Inside because these ministry programs are being brought to the inmate population that is incarcerated inside of the prisons.

Kairos Outside began in 1989 when a chaplain at San Quentin State Correctional Facility in California asked Kairos to create programming for the female family members of those incarcerated. In April of 1990, their first meeting was held in Northern California.

It did not stop there. Kairos Torch was formed in 1997 for youth twenty-five years old and younger who are incarcerated, and there is also a program for female prisoners.

It is unbelievable what Kairos Prison Ministries has grown into and the amazing impact they have made and are still making. They operate with a staff of eleven and have over 30,000 volunteers who are donating three million hours of service per year. Volunteers are from independent and non-denominational churches and others. They serve more than 400 correctional institutions in eighty-six communities in thirty-seven states and nine countries: Costa Rica, Australia, Canada, Dominican Republic, Honduras, Nicaragua, Peru, South Africa, and the United Kingdom.

As you can find on their website or read about them, the positive impact Kairos has achieved is well documented.

The following is taken from their website:

> Prison is a dark, hopeless place. Prisoners often live their lives without friends, without family, staring at the prison bars and feeling guilt and anger burning in their hearts.

> Spouses, parents, and relatives of the incarcerated often "do time" right along with their loved ones, feeling alone and guilty. Through the work of over 30,000 volunteers, Kairos Prison Ministry brings the light, love, and friendship of Jesus Christ into their lives. They know they are forgiven, and they know they are loved. It is truly a life-changing and often life-sav-

ing experience.

Hearts are changed, prisons are less violent, recidi-
vism rates are reduced, and communities are safer.

I wanted to share this part of my life with others for unselfish
reasons. I know what hopelessness and darkness feel like, and I
wanted to reach out to others. I want others to know that if you
are at the bottom of the barrel like I was, believe that you are
not without hope. You can get through it. Try to picture yourself
swimming to the top of the barrel and crawling out of it. Pray
and believe, because I am living proof that God does answer your
prayers. I felt at one point in my life that I was worthless and no
one would care whether I lived or died. I am so grateful to have
been spared. I am not without problems or issues in my life, but I
have a reason to go on, to live out the rest of the days in my life,
and strive every day to be better. To make it count.

To help to make it better for others.

Chapter Thirteen:

There Was Pain and There Was Laughter

ANNA MARIE'S INTERVIEW AND STORY.

I started playing tennis at an early age. Right off the bat, I was told that I had a

natural ability for the sport. To share a little bit about playing tennis: it is very much a physical

sport that requires the use of every muscle group in your body. You not only have to be strong, you also need to possess and have long-lasting stamina and endurance. Tennis is also very much a mental game because you have to be able to think quickly so that you are able to determine what your best shot is. To dominate in the game, you have to strategize using your best, quick, and powerful thinking skills so that you are both faster and better than your opponent. When you play the match strategically, you know when it is just the perfect time to use your overhead smash against your opponent. I had that combination: power, determination, and body strength.

The potential and talent that I had were obvious to the coach at the tennis club where my parents had signed me up to take lessons.

I started training at the age of twelve, and my mother worked at the tennis club to help pay for my lessons. My personal tennis coach's name was Bill, and he was the pro at the club. Under his expert coaching skills, it was obvious that I was advancing quickly. He was very pleased with both my abilities and my progress. My parents were more than well-pleased with the progress I was making. For all of us, my parents, my coach, and myself, a special friendship started to grow.

Bill was married with children. At the age of fourteen or fifteen, I began babysitting for him and his wife's children. I adored their children, and they adored me. We all became very close with each other. In fact, we became so close that our families started spending many of the holidays together. My parents really liked Bill, and they were very appreciative of the special interest that he took in me. Bill had such a dynamic personality. It was easy to see that under his coaching I was on my way to becoming a top-notch tennis player. The lessons that my parents were paying for were most definitely paying off.

When I was about the age of sixteen, I started traveling with Bill to attend tennis clinics. I would work alongside him as his assistant to help with training other athletes. He was well respected for his expertise as a top-notch tennis pro coach. Bill was seventeen years older than me.

In tennis, the game starts at "love", which means 0–0. We began *at* love, and then we fell *in* love. When I was sixteen, not only was Bill my coach, but he became my lover. I was sure that

I was in love with him, and he said that he loved me, too.

As you can imagine, this became a very difficult time for my family once they found out. My parents were devastated because they liked Bill, and they trusted him. They felt that they had been deceived, lied to, and were made fools of. They felt betrayed. They also blamed me. So, because of this situation, my parents did not speak to me or have any contact whatsoever with me for a little over two years. That time in my life was so hard. My heart ached. I deeply loved my parents.

Bill's wife found out about the affair much later. It wasn't until I was away at college that Bill asked his wife for a divorce. He then moved out of his house so that he could be closer to me. To me, it did not seem like our affair and his divorce were all that hard on Bill's children. I think the reason for this was because his children and I had grown so close over all the years that I had spent with them and babysitting. Even though I am sure they were shocked when they first found this out. It had to be awkward for them. But we still had a close relationship.

Bill and I remained together as a couple for about thirteen years. He was terribly possessive with me, and he was extremely jealous. When I was away at another college because I was working on my master's degree, he would drive three and half hours, showing up completely unannounced, just to try and catch me cheating on him. I wasn't cheating on him, and I never did, but he always suspected that I was. He was very controlling. He felt that he owned me, like I was his very own personal possession.

He was also extremely abusive to me. His temper was frightening.

One time, when we were in the car together, he became so angry with me that he threw me out of the car and left me alone in a ghetto-like and very run-down area and then just drove away. I was terrified, to say the least. I was lost and without any means to get myself home except to walk. He had left me stranded several miles from our home.

He had carefully groomed me right from the beginning. His grooming started when I was at the age of twelve. He always felt that he owned and controlled me. He had such a dynamic

personality, and I thought he was exciting to be around. He was very different from the father role that I had grown up with.

The very positive thing that I got out of this relationship is that he pushed me to be better at everything that I did. He pushed me to be better at tennis, and he pushed me to further my education. I received scholarships for my degrees, and it was because of his pushing me to

excel and to always apply myself to achieve my very best. We were a fun couple, too. We laughed, we danced; he even introduced me to some of the finer things in life, like good wine. I learned what the best labels were and how to compare the different wine tastes, the origins, and the vintages. I became very much a sophisticated wine snob.

Our sex life was exciting, and it seemed like we could never get enough of each other. Which is why I was completely shocked when I found out, years later, that he had cheated on me.

The two years that my family had disowned me, those years were extremely hard and sad times for me. I hated that I had disappointed my family. I loved them, and I felt bad that they felt that I had let them down and hurt them. My parents and family are still now, and always have been, very important to me. The only reason that we eventually reconnected was because my grandfather died. He was my mother's father, and my parents wanted me to come home for the funeral. It is times like this that make us realize how important our family truly is.

After my grandfather died, my family and I started to come back together. But our getting

together did not include Bill. Whenever I would visit my parents, Bill would have to drop me off at the corner from my parents' house so that they would not see him. My parents had written him off as someone they could no longer trust. By this time, Bill had taken another pro tennis coaching job at a country club. It was close to the university that I was attending. He always felt that he had to stay in close proximity to wherever I was so that he would always know what I was doing and who I was talking to.

His abuse and his temper were frightening. A few times when he was beating me, I got scared, and I called the police. But I never formally pressed charges against him. One time, he choked me around my neck so hard that the necklace that I was wearing broke in half, and I was left desperately gasping for air. I was very close to passing out and losing consciousness.

All of that did not matter to me. I still cared for and loved him regardless. I was under his

spell. I was somewhere between twenty-four years old and twenty-six when Bill told me that it was over between us, and he wanted me to get out. He had been cheating on me for a long time, and I was sure that I knew it, but he kept denying it. I was so desperate not to lose him that I never pressed it. I don't think I would have ever broken it off between us. At this point, he was the only man that I had ever had in my life, starting at the immature age of twelve. I could not even begin to imagine what my life would be like without him. He was my coach, he was my guy, and he was my lover.

After we parted ways, I felt lost until I met another man who was seven years younger than me. His name was Rob. He was so much different than Bill. He was extremely good-looking; he was kind, and he was gentle. After the breakup with Bill, I was going through a wild and reckless time in my life. I was trying to figure out who I was and where I was going.

My meeting Rob and being with him brought a gentle calmness into my life. This calmness and gentleness were something that I had never had before.

Bill, for whatever reasons, ended his relationship with the

woman that he had left me for. So, he then wanted and expected that we would get back together. He started treating me the same way he always had. He was abusive, demanding, and insistent on how things should be between us. I think I found his behavior to be normal. I had lived with this behavior for so many years. It is all I really knew. I thought his aggression was proof to me of just how much he loved and wanted me.

Bill's persistent pushing and trying to gain control over me did not win out this time. I resisted, and I chose to be with Rob instead. Rob and I decided to get married, and we were together for the next four years. He was so warm and kind to me. Besides his good looks, he was such a passionate lover. I hadn't ever experienced that kind of passion and gentleness in bed before. He treated me gently, respectfully, and he always spoke softly and kindly to me. He told

me how much he loved me all the time. He made me feel special.

Sadly, I ended up cheating on him. I truly, to this day, still feel bad about that. But I became so bored with him, and I did not feel happy. Rob was not at all exciting to be with. He was so passive and low-key. He was such a homebody and just not my type. He was not abusive, which I am grateful for. So, in reality, I know that he was good for me. But he was happy to just sit at home and watch TV. I was so bored that I bought a ping-pong table, thinking it would get him out of his chair. He also wanted to have kids, and that was a big "no" for me. I really did not want my own children. So, all this boredom caused me to start looking for something more,

something exciting. I started going out and partying with the guys that I worked with. Faithful and loving Rob sat at home while I was out. He was always happy to see me when I came home. No matter how late it was.

On one occasion, while I was out partying, I was roofied while I was at a hockey game. That was a wild and scary time and experience for me. I am not entirely sure what happened to me that night. I lost my purse, so I had no money. I was looking for a cab to get a ride home. I don't know how I thought I was going to be able to pay for a cab. Luckily for me, a girl saw that I looked afraid and lost. She offered to drive me home, which was more than an hour away. I will always be grateful to her, this stranger who rescued me. This could have turned out very badly for me. I shudder to think what else could have possibly happened to me that night. I was in a dangerous and vulnerable situation.

Of course, my parents loved Rob. They could see that he was a stable influence on me. But I was with him just long enough for me to be able to label our time together as a short cooling-off period and a dull chapter in my life. I wanted a divorce, and I wanted some excitement in my life. Sitting at home watching TV was not my idea of spending quality and fun time together.

While going through my divorce, I met a guy at a country

club one evening while

attending a social event with a girlfriend. He was a fireman, which, for me, added an element of danger. I guess I thought that you had to be brave and daring to be a fireman and a rescue person. I was sure that danger didn't scare him. He was also a big golfer, and he had a big personality that always made him the center of attention wherever he was. He was not at all quiet or reserved. He was nothing like Rob. He was not the best-looking, but he sure thought he was cool and quite the ladies' man.

Confidence just oozed out of him. People liked just being around him. It was like he

was some kind of big shot or celebrity. My girlfriend introduced us. At this same time, she had a

thing for him. So, needless to say, my starting a relationship with this new guy, Jared, caused a

falling out between myself and my friend.

Soon, Jared was taking control of my life. He took up tennis and not so that we

could enjoy playing together. No, not at all. He wanted to crush me and beat me on the court. He wanted to reign superior over me. I was not allowed to have any activity in my life that did not include him. He always had to be the best, better, and superior in everything we did. I would quickly learn that he was the superior and most important person in this relationship. It was definitely not me.

I did not heed all these warnings, and I ignored all the red flags. Foolishly, I moved in

with him. It seemed like a good thing at the time. He had a nice house, and he had a lot of friends. Such a big life he lived compared to being married to Rob. And he was closer to my age. He was only four years older than me. I thought this would help make a positive difference in our relationship after being with and married to a much younger man.

As far as he was concerned, I could not do anything right. He was constantly correcting me and diminishing me. One time, he threw me down our stairs during one of his violent rages. I was sitting quietly working on my computer on some of my college class work when suddenly he lunged at me and started accusing me of cheating on him. He picked me up and threw me hard down the stairs. I was in a lot of pain, so he had to take me to the hospital emergency room. The X-rays showed that I had suffered broken ribs and I had contusions. Of course, he felt bad. He always felt bad after he hurt me. So, his way to always try to make everything better after one of his violent episodes was that we would go for ice cream.

So, after we left the hospital and he told me over and over again how sorry he was, we went for ice cream. Ice cream was going to make everything better.

The hospital prescribed pain pills for me because I was in a lot of pain. He ended up stealing those pills from me. So much for my needing the pills to help with my pain. He just let me suffer, and it did not affect or bother him at all.

Our neighbors would look out on our front lawn after a night of his yelling, raging, fighting,

and abuse and see that all of my clothes had been thrown out of the bedroom window.

Whenever he was gone, I was not allowed to leave our house. I would take my phone out to the curb directly in front of our house. I would put my phone in my mailbox and then sit on the curb directly across the street from our neighbors. This way, I was not leaving my house because I was not allowed to. This was the only way that I could talk to my neighbors. If he called, I could grab the phone from the mailbox, and he wouldn't know that I was outside talking with the neighbors.

I was finishing up my PhD for school when we met. He had to know everything I did. He was insanely jealous. He picked out the clothes that I wore. He told me what my ideal weight was for my height and bone structure and that I had better exercise and diet to achieve that weight, and then I had better maintain it. He was sexually abusive. He liked it rough. The rougher, the better. He liked to cause pain. It was a better climax for him to hear my pleading for him to stop because he was hurting me. He liked hearing my cries of "please, stop." He liked my begging.

As a fireman working at the station, if he was not out on a

call, he watched porn at the station all day long. Whatever porn he watched, he then wanted to try to have that same sex with me. He wanted to imitate all of it. There was nothing tender about satisfying him sexually, and it was definitely not lovemaking. It was raw and savage-like. It was brutal even. I was not allowed to have any friends. And when he worked his twenty-four-hour shift, he demanded and expected that I go to the fire station to give him sex.

After he broke my ribs, I decided that I had to get out of our relationship. I felt he might possibly end up killing me. I did leave him, but it was hard to keep him away. A few times, he threatened suicide, and on one occasion, he attempted it, and he came very close to dying.

While I was still healing from my broken ribs, I met another guy. On the exact day that we met, he had put out a "For Sale" sign in his yard in front of his house. He was selling his home because he had found out, that very day, that his wife had cheated on him. So, here we were, two broken people who happened to meet each other. It ended up that those two broken people married each other. Today, we are still together.

My husband Tony is so well grounded. He truly is a good match for me after everything that I have been through. Neither of us wants to go through the hurt and pain that we both have

experienced in our previous relationships.

Tony comes from a close Italian family. I also come from a

strong Italian family. If you know anything about Italian culture, you know that family (*la famiglia*) is what is most important. Close family relationships, respect, and support are expected and instilled in you, starting at a very young age. Family loyalty is huge.

While my current husband, Tony, and I were dating, Jared was stalking me. He had such bizarre, unstable behavior. Like painting mean faces on golf balls and then leaving them in our yard. He actually met and made friends with our neighbors who lived directly behind us just so that he could spy on me. I often shudder remembering some of his bizarre and scary behavior. Once, while we were vacationing in the Bahamas, he became so terribly angry with me over something stupid that he abandoned me in the downtown area. Anything could have happened to me, and he simply did not care. He was always mad at me about something, and it did not matter what it was. He was always ready to pick a fight just so that he could punish me and hurt me. And after he hurt me, he would then want to have makeup sex.

But even the sex was abusive and painful. His porn addiction made him crazy and dangerous because he wanted to inflict pain on me to satisfy his crazy sexual needs. If it wasn't violent, he wouldn't be satisfied.

At one point, while I was dating Tony, my current husband, Jared, was in the hospital. Jared kept calling me and begging me to please come to the hospital and visit him. He sounded so desperate, and I felt sorry for him. For whatever reason, I felt it was cruel not to go to see him. I cannot truly explain how he had this effect and control over me. After all the pain and hurt he inflicted on me, why did I care? I knew I should not trust him. This was his way of always roping me back in. It was his pattern of manipulating me. His narcissistic behavior was dangerous.

He was eventually released from his job at the fire department for mental health reasons. I think I might have been close to death more than once during our time together. Why did I stay as long as I did? Why did I let him hurt and abuse me the way that he did? What does that say about me? I think I just don't see the controlling and harmful signs in others until I am already involved, and then I am trapped.

My marriage to Tony did have a rough start. On our wedding day, he became angry with me for having a glass of wine with my sister before the wedding. It was just one glass of wine, but he was upset with me, and this was our special wedding day. He hurt my feelings, and I cried at the altar during our vows. For our honeymoon night, I slept in the closet because he had made such a big deal out of it. So, our supposed-to-be-romantic honeymoon in Italy was ten whole days of me crying because I felt Tony had ruined our wedding. He was supposed to be my guy. And to make matters worse, my own mother sided with him. Even to this day, my family sides with him over everything.

I am the oldest child in our family. I have a brother and sister who married their high school sweethearts. They are both considered to be my parents' good children. I am the black sheep of the family. Maybe they feel that way because of my grandfather. My grandfather was an alcoholic, and he was abusive. They feel there is some bad blood that flows in our family. They think that, possibly, some bad blood runs through my veins. But for the most part, I have been a victim. I also know and admit that I have faults. My mother said to Tony, on the day of our wedding, that he still had time to back out if he wanted to. Thanks, Mom! But Tony didn't back out, and he is here with me, and he is my steady. I am content, and I have a good life. It took me a long time to get here. It took me a long time to find him.

If I could share words of advice or words of comfort for others, I would start by saying you deserve better. No one deserves to be diminished, beaten, and controlled. Stop looking for the bigger-than-life guy. Because that guy truly only loves himself, and you are just an object to him. You are someone who can be easily discarded. I never wanted to be alone, so I jumped from one relationship to another.

I have asked myself why did all of this happen to me over the years. I started out being a promising tennis star. I was strong. I had stamina and determination. I had developed a strong mental capability. I learned to dominate and strategize to beat my opponent. I knew the perfect time to play my overhead smash. And then, somehow, all that special talent and strength and determination was stripped from me, and I became easily manipulated. A calculated, controlling power took over and stole my confidence. I became someone very different from the person who trained and worked hard and started out to be. I know that I am a good and caring person, but trust is very hard for me. The emotional and physical scars that I have endured shook my core and damaged my confidence. It took a big bite out of my life that I can't get back. So, going forward, I want to use my life experiences as very hard lessons learned and to not ever go down that path again. Thank goodness for my long-lasting stamina that I started out with while I was in training because otherwise, I might not have survived.

I relate to the lyrics in the song "When I Was Young" by Eric Burdon & The Animals. I related to the lyrics about innocence, nostalgia, and being carefree when I was young. Later in life, I relate to my longing for those carefree days and reflecting on it all.

Chapter Fourteen:

"Fight or Flight" Is How I Lived Most of My Life

KATIE'S INTERVIEW AND STORY.

Our all-important response and reaction when we are faced with danger is the fight-or-flight mode our body goes into. I am seventy years old, and, as I reflect over my life, there is so much that has happened to me that I can't even believe that I am actually still alive. The number of times that I thought my life was over is a number I don't want to add up. And for what reasons would I want to? I can't change or take back anything that happened. None of us can erase the pain and hurt from our past.

So, life for me today is much quieter. I try to stay in the shadows. I isolate myself because it feels safer. I am so very tired from fighting the fight to survive that began for me when I was just about four years old.

My real father was an alcoholic and a womanizer. He fathered seven children with my mother, and I am the oldest. Five girls and two boys. Who knows how many other children he might have fathered as well. One of my brothers died when he was a baby. My dad, for the most part, was not a full-time resident in our home. That was his choice. There are many times I remember that he would say that he was going out to get a pack of cigarettes or to pick something up from the store, and we would not see him again for sometimes a month. Sometimes even longer. And when he did show back up, he would tell my mom how much he loved her and missed her. I think all that love he showered on her convinced her he was sorry. She would forgive him and love him back, and they would disappear into the bedroom. Soon after all that forgiveness and love, my mom would be pregnant again and another baby was on the way. This pattern continued until we had five little kids in the house. On some mornings, when we all woke up, if our dad had been gone for a while, there would be little or sometimes no food at all in the house for us to eat.

By the time I turned seven and I was going to school, my mother was at a breaking point. She had five hungry little children to feed. One morning, my mom wrote a note to her dad begging him for help. At the time, we lived in a farmhouse out in the country, quite a distance from town. My grandparents lived in that small town. We did not have a phone at the farmhouse. So, my mom told me to run across the field to our neighbor's house and give them the note that she had written for her dad. She knew that the neighbors did have a phone. My mom had written her dad's phone number on the outside of the note, and when I handed the note to the neighbors, I explained it was important. They called my grandparents, and soon after, my grandparents showed up at the farmhouse.

Her father told her that he would help. He said he would get her a house so that we would be closer to them. And he would help with the bills. But he had one firm stipulation that she had to agree to. It was that she could not allow her no-good husband back in the house ever again. So, we made that move to the house that was closer to them. But my dad didn't care about the rules and stipulations that my grandfather had made. My dad still showed up whenever he wanted. And when he came, he would always tell us how much he loved and missed my mother and us kids. He just couldn't stay away. That always made us feel special, even if it was short-lived.

Although there was a lot of turmoil at home, I still managed to be a good student in school. It brings a smile to my face when I recall a proud moment I had at school. I was about the age of eight or nine years old. I was the only student in my class that knew all the states and all the capitals in each state. I was also the only student that got an A+. Boy, was I happy with myself. I don't remember my dad being around to see that. I wish he would have been.

The house that we had moved to that my grandfather rented for us was very close to the railroad yard in the small town that we lived in. I am not sure if the trains spilled grains or cereals, which attracted rodents, but it was a big problem around and in our house. One of my sisters, who was at the time still a baby and slept in a crib, was bitten by a rat. She had to have rabies shots, which I am sure was awful, and she was very sick. But the rabies shots saved her life.

It was unacceptable for us to stay living in that house, for fear something like this might happen again. My mom started looking for somewhere else for us to live. Even though I loved my school and did not want to leave it, I understood why we had to. I did not want any of my siblings to get bitten by another rat. So, we packed up our belongings, and we moved out of the small town we loved. We found a small house in another town, and I would be starting to go to a brand-new school.

I do not remember playing much at all as a child, nor do I remember having any friends. My memory is that I was always helping with my younger siblings. I felt more like a mother to them than I did a sister. After we were settled into our new house, my mom started showing interest in another man who lived in the neighborhood. Unfortunately, he was married. But I know, at the age that I was, I did not have any concerns or questions about any of it. I do not remember questioning my mom about this at all. Besides, I was busy babysitting and going to school, and who knew for sure how marriage was supposed to even look like or how it was supposed to be. My experience with my dad was that the husband and father would not be around much. He would leave for weeks or months at a time. He would drink till he was drunk, and there would be a lot of yelling and fighting. That was our normal, and that is what I knew. All of this could have been completely normal about the guy down the street. I thought maybe he was like a substitute dad.

My mom would write notes to this neighbor man that she

liked, and she would put them in an envelope. Then she would ask me to walk the note, which smelled of perfume, down to his house and put it in his mailbox. All these years later, I still wonder about the fact; wasn't that all a bit risky on her part? Especially since he was married. How did his wife not find out? Did she never check the mailbox? Or did she know?

My mom was also working part-time, close to our house. Money was tight, and there were lots of mouths to feed. At some point, while we were living in this house, my mother was turned in for child neglect by a hateful sister-in-law. She never liked my mother. But the actions that she took against my mother accelerated an already bad situation and turned our lives into a complete living nightmare for years and years after.

Our mother went to prison because of it, all five of us kids were turned over to child services, and then each of us was put into foster homes. And not the good kind of foster homes. The kind of homes that leave scars on you for the rest of your life. There were only two of us out of five children who managed to be put in a good foster home.

The day we went to court and our mom was sentenced to prison, all five of us kids were dressed up in new clothes and new shoes. We were spic-and-span from head to toe. The social worker handling our case had taken care of this. She was making sure we did not look like neglected, ragamuffin children on our day in court in front of the judge. We all looked very nice, and we practiced our good manners. But I remember that my little brother had a pair of shoes that were way too small for his feet, and the shoes were hurting him. He was about five years old. I remember him sobbing and crying because his feet hurt so bad. But he was such a little trooper because he wanted to look his best in front of the judge to help our mom. So, he fought back his tears. I was so proud of that little guy that day. He was doing his duty and his part to help our mom.

My mother was pregnant when she went into prison, and she gave that baby up for adoption. It was a baby girl. I was told that the court stepped in and told her that she had to make a choice. She could either give up her children, who were currently in foster care, or she could give up her newborn baby. She chose to give up the baby. What a hard decision for a mother to have to make.

When our mom was released from prison after serving her time, she was on probation. She had to follow court orders after her release. She had to have a job and an acceptable home that was able to house the five children before she could even try to get her kids back. She took a job at a diner in the small town that she grew up in. While working there, she met a truck driver. She was charmed by him and all the special attention that he showered her with. Before long, he asked her to marry him. He also made a promise to her to help raise her five children. It is safe to say that my mother picked two of the worst possible men to fall in love with and then marry. It is also safe to say that she lived almost all her life in a very bad place, suffering a lot of hurt and pain. Happiness was definitely not in her vocabulary or in her life. If there were any high points, they were very short-lived.

The life choices that she made and what her bad choices meant for us kids would forever scar us. We had a mostly absent alcoholic father. Because of that, we were poor and neglected. Our stepfather turned out to be a sexual abuser of all of us kids and a verbal abuser, too; he relentlessly beat us almost daily and sometimes beat us almost to our deaths. He also beat my mother, and sometimes those beatings were so bad that she was not even recognizable.

All five of us grew up believing we were stupid, ugly, worthless, and we would never amount to anything. We heard and lived that nightmare every single day.

Our stepfather moved all of us to another state. He then put my mother and all of us kids to work at the motel truck stop that he had purchased. For a long time, my mother was not aware of our sexual abuse, but even when she did find out, she was helpless to stop it. To stop any of it. Sexual abuse and beatings. He constantly threatened all of us with her going back to prison and then all of us going back to an orphanage if we ever told anyone. When they married, I was about the age of twelve. It was not until I turned the age of sixteen that I was able to escape. During those years in between, I thought about all the ways that I could kill him. The scars from all the beatings are still visible all these years later and a painful reminder of our lives. My mother, my siblings, and myself were tied up and beaten with some of the most unthinkable punishment objects that could inflict pain on us. To keep us in line. To remind us that he was in control of everything in our life. Fight-or-flight was in our constant consciousness. Our legs, arms, and back had lacerations that we had to hide under long sleeves and pants so that our teachers would not ask questions. And if they did ask why your face was all bruised up, you had a ready-made lie you had to tell. If not, the next beating would be even worse, and your mother and other siblings would pay for it, too. No one was safe. No one was special. Except for a baby brother that my mother and stepfather had.

When I moved out to escape the nightmare that we were all living in, there were times that I would see how badly he was still beating my siblings. A few times, I went to the police. I do not know if he was paying off the police or they just did not believe me, but nothing ever happened to him, and it only made it worse for all of us. If they did investigate, the kids were threatened to not tell the truth, or they would be sorry. And so, the police would come, and then they would go. Nothing happened. Can you imagine living a life like this? You are hoping and praying that someone is going to help you, rescue you, and then the rescuer leaves, and nothing happens, and now you know you are going to pay the price. This is what hopelessness looks like. I could paint you a vivid picture of hopelessness. It is the face in the mirror that I would see every day. It is the face of my siblings and my mother. The tears that had stopped flowing because, after a while, you started to feel numb. It was hopeless, and you did not care anymore.

I remember all the supermen heroes on shows that were supposed to come "to save the day." Superman never came to our house.

I know some people were definitely afraid of him. He seemed to have this power, and people feared him. Some people acted like he was a big shot, someone important. I just wanted him to die. I wished for this all the time, and I am not ashamed to say it.

My family left the truck stop business and moved to Kentucky. I stayed back because, at the time, I was married. But I stayed in touch as much as possible. At one point, one of my sisters moved back when she turned sixteen. She made her escape as soon as she could, too. She had called her high school sweetheart to come pick her up, and they decided to get married. He was in the military, so they packed up and moved to the military base.

I have always felt like a failure. Not good enough. I do not ever remember being praised for anything. So, I made some really bad choices in some of the men in my life. My mother was not a good role model. I've been married four times, and only one of those was good. My second husband attempted to kill me several times. His favorite chosen method was to choke me. There were many times that I was within seconds of dying. Sometimes, I would lose consciousness. One time, he threw me through a picture window.

The beatings were getting worse, and I was at a breaking

point. Even though I knew moving back in with my mom and stepfather was not a good choice, I had nowhere else to turn. My husband was going to end up killing me if I did not get away.

I was shocked when I arrived in Kentucky, and I saw how they were all living. There was no running water and no electricity. They lived high up on a mountain. It was like they were twenty years behind the times. Fortunately, I was able to quickly find a job so that I could get out and on my own. The sooner, the better; nothing had changed. My stepfather was still beating the family and sexually and verbally abusing them.

While living and working in Kentucky I met my third husband, and with him, I had two children. He was a good provider.

I had a baby with my first husband. Sadly, our baby died. They ruled it a crib death. I cannot begin to tell you the hurt and pain that you go through when you lose a precious child.

I have regrets about my moving to that part of Kentucky. The lifestyle back then, I think, left my children without high expectations and accepting a lifestyle that did not turn out to be the best for them. Even though they were given plenty of love, they were well provided for, they were not beaten, and we tried our best with them. But they settled for little out of life. They did not always connect with the right people, and they sometimes did not make some very good choices. I know what a mother is supposed to look like, so I really tried to be good at it. I also know what a mother is not supposed to look like. Your surroundings and your environment do influence your life and the choices that you make. Some people are fortunate enough to see that there are better choices, and they want a better future for themselves, so they make the move. They escape.

My fourth husband was the only one who was truly good to me, and he died from a sudden heart attack. That's when you start to question why. When is it enough? Why did this happen? Was this truly my lot in life?

At one point in my life, I attempted suicide and almost succeeded. I remember that I thought that everything in my life was hopeless and killing myself would stop the pain.

I only have one good Christmas memory as a child. It was the year that one of my sisters and I got a pair of white go-go boots and a mohair sweater. Boy, do I remember that day and the feelings of excitement and happiness. I sure thought we were the cat's meow. Christmas is such a special time many children look forward to. I think Santa only came once. But the excitement about the boots and sweater was short-lived. It turned out not to be a good day at our house. In fact, I was asked when we were interviewing and writing for this book what happy childhood memories I could share. I thought hard, and I honestly drew a blank. I know there are others who have suffered, and when they look back, nothing comes to mind for them either. It is not supposed to be that way.

For most of my life, I was always looking for something better, but sadly I never found it. And it is not because I didn't try. So, at some point in my life, I just quit hoping for it, and I quit expecting it. I just settled for where I was and what I had because I believed that this was as good as it was going to get.

I do not believe that my mother ever made any good decisions. Even at the end of her life, she dealt us another hard blow. I took beatings for my mother all through the years to protect her. I cleaned and cooked and watched over my siblings. I loved her and cared for her. My mother passed on now several years ago. My stepfather died before her. Because she is my mother, I will always love her. And I forgive her for the hurt and pain that she caused for all of us, the bad decisions that she made, and for not getting us out and saving us from the horrible evil we lived with after she married our stepfather. But what breaks my heart even more is that when my mother died, and speaking only for myself, I was not even mentioned in her will.

I cannot reason or grasp why that was, and it hurts.

What also happened when my mom was sick and dying in the hospital was that she had designated my half-brother's wife as her medical decision-maker. My siblings and I were shocked and hurt. She was our mother, not hers. We had been at our mother's side after our stepdad died, always carefully caring for her and helping her, even financially, whenever we could at every turn. I do not have answers for so many of the choices that my mother made. And so many of her choices deeply and negatively affected our lives forever.

What I am passionate about is making people aware of all kinds of abuse and helping children who are trapped in hopeless situations. To make people more aware of the foster care system that desperately needs more help and major changes. There are so many helpless victims out there. Maybe this is part of my purpose, and I survived all that I did to be able to tell my story and to be able to give hope to others. To wake up and shake up the people who look away and say to them, "Pay attention. Look for the signs of neglect and abuse because you could be saving a life."

I pray that, in some way, I have helped someone.

You need to have courage, stay hopeful and have faith, even at the times in your life when you think God is not listening. When you think no one cares.

Chapter Fifteen:

I Put Them First Before Myself for Everything

CATHERINE'S INTERVIEW AND STORY.

I was born and raised in Ohio, and I am the oldest of three children. I would describe my life growing up as coming from a lower-middle-class and religious family. My childhood was filled with lots of rock and roll and country music. I have been in love with music and singing for as long as I can remember. In fact, I taught myself how to sing and play the guitar. I have never had any formal lessons.

My parents were worship leaders in our church. That is, until my grandfather died. Then it seemed like everything changed. At that time, I was twelve years old. Sadly, after my grandfather died, my dad gave up playing the guitar and singing. From that point on, we only attended our church as members and no longer as leaders.

I am a divorced mother with two young children. My daughter is thirteen, and my son is eleven years old. They are absolutely the love and pride of my life. I put them first before myself for everything.

My parents' faith is paramount in how they live their lives

and how they believe all their family should live their lives. My daughter struggles with her grandmother's overbearing preaching all the time. My mother worries about all of us going to hell, so she is constantly preaching and praying for us. I always remind my mother that I know that she worries and loves us, but my daughter is thirteen years old, and all this preaching is a lot for her to have to deal with.

I am reminded of a time growing up when I was in my sixth-grade music class. I was seated next to a bully who harassed me for the entire school year. He would not let me hold the sheet music, and he would not share it with me either, even though he was supposed to. I always had to share with two other boys. One day in class, I finally managed to get the upper hand. That made him mad, and he became so angry that he was being verbally nasty to me. I just could not hold my anger back any longer. At that point, I had enough! So, I stood up to him. I shouted out for him to, "Shut the hell up!"

The teacher at my school almost gave me a detention for this, but said if I wrote a letter of apology, she would not punish me. But worse than the potential detention, I was in more trouble with my parents. I had said the word "hell," and for that, I would be learning a lesson that I was sure to never ever forget. My punishment was that I had to handwrite the verse Psalm 51 from the Bible five times, memorize it, and recite it word for word. While standing in front of my parents, if I missed reciting more than five of the words, I would have to start all over again with the entire punishment. That included rewriting it, too. I did not completely understand the fairness of my being punished. Although I knew I should not have used that word. But I was defending and standing up for myself. I think that was a good thing.

As you can read for yourself, Psalm 51 is the longest verse in the Bible. It is a hymn and a scripture that was supposed to cleanse my heart, and God would then have mercy on me. This was because I was evil, I was born sinful, and I had been sinful from the time that my mother conceived me, and I needed to be cleansed.

> Have mercy on me, O God,
> according to your unfailing love;
> according to your great compassion
> blot out my transgressions.
> Wash away all my iniquity
> and cleanse me from my sin.
>
> For I know my transgressions,
> and my sin is always before me.
> Against you, you only, have I sinned
> and done what is evil in your sight;
> so you are right in your verdict
> and justified when you judge.
> Surely I was sinful at birth,
> sinful from the time my mother conceived me.
> Yet you desired faithfulness even in the womb;
> you taught me wisdom in that secret place.

Cleanse me with hyssop, and I will be clean;

wash me, and I will be whiter than snow.

Let me hear joy and gladness;

let the bones you have crushed rejoice.

Hide your face from my sins

and blot out all my iniquity.

Create in me a pure heart, O God,

and renew a steadfast spirit within me.

Do not cast me from your presence

or take your Holy Spirit from me.

Restore to me the joy of your salvation

and grant me a willing spirit, to sustain me.

Then I will teach transgressors your ways,

so that sinners will turn back to you.

Deliver me from the guilt of bloodshed, O God,

you who are God, my Savior,

and my tongue will sing of your righteousness.

Open my lips, Lord,

and my mouth will declare your praise.

You do not delight in sacrifice, or I would bring it;

you do not take pleasure in burnt offerings.

My sacrifice, O God, is a broken spirit;

a broken and contrite heart

you, God, will not despise.

May it please you to prosper Zion,

to build up the walls of Jerusalem.

Then you will delight in the sacrifices of the righteous,

in burnt offerings offered whole;

then bulls will be offered on your altar.

Psalm 51 (NIV)

My dad was abusive, and he believed in corporal punishment. The physical abuse was beyond spanking. I would see the unfairness of how my siblings and I were being treated and how he would go overboard with his temper and punishments. He would get so red in the face and so angry that he was actually spitting in our faces as he was yelling. When my siblings did something wrong, even though I had done nothing wrong, it did not matter. I was in trouble, too. It was not fair, and so, I would say so. I couldn't help it; I had to speak up. But it didn't matter, and it only made it worse for me. I was about the age of fourteen or fifteen when I started speaking up. I remember one time looking in the mirror after my dad hit me and seeing a bright red imprint on my face where he slapped me. This hard slap was my punishment for speaking up. My brother and sister always stood silent and watched. They were afraid to say anything. They would see what was happening to me. They are both still like that today. They never make waves or speak up for themselves. Over the years, my mom has told me that I am different: I am tiger-blooded.

When I was a young teenager in school, and we had a Fun Friday, like a dress-up pajama day, I would never be allowed to participate. My parents felt that it wasn't appropriate, so I was not allowed. It is hard to feel like you fit in with everybody else when you are not allowed to even participate in a Fun Friday. It was just pajamas.

In all my years growing up, I suffered many physical punishments from my father. My mom, on the other hand, would just haul off and hit us kids with anything that she could find. It could be a hairbrush, a bottle of water, a shoe, or whatever. She was also big into shaming us. I was taught that my whole purpose and existence was to serve, to please, and to care for others. We had very strict rules to abide by. There was constant judgment and a lot of critical commentary on how I should dress and act. From the moment we got home from school every day, we had a long list of chores we each had to complete. If we didn't finish the chores, we were punished. It included making dinner, vacuuming the entire house and stairs, caring for the animals we had, dishes, etc. From the moment my parents got home from work, we became servants. If my parents wanted anything, like coffee, a snack, etc., we were expected to drop what we were doing, including homework, to give them what they wanted. That included being a human remote control for the TV well into my teen years.

In our house, it was "Spare the rod, spoil the child," like in Proverbs 13:24: "Whoever spares the rod hates their children, but the one who loves their children is careful to discipline them."

I have never spanked my kids. I promised myself early on that I would not treat my children like my parents treated me. I would be better. I would do better. I tell my children that I am sorry whenever I feel that I could have handled something better than I did. For me, as a child growing up, if I could have gotten one apology from either my mom or my dad, it would have gone a long way in helping with how I felt about a lot of things.

The first chance I could, at age fifteen-and-a-half, I got a job at a grocery store just to be able to get out of the house. I would be in school all day, and then I went straight from there to work until it closed at 8:00 p.m. When I went to college, I commuted because we could not afford for me to live on campus. Again, I would stay at school and away from my home and parents as late and as much as possible.

I was working for a graphic design company when I met my husband. He came in to order something. Right away, he was friendly, and he really seemed to take a special interest in me, and he was also my age. Up until that time, all the guys that had shown any interest in me were always older. Because of my religious upbringing, I had been taught, and I had always believed that there would be just one special person in my life. I believed that this person was put on this earth specially for me. I was taught that God brings us together to meet our soul mate. So, I took this meeting on that day as a direct sign from God. Well, it was a sign, all right, but what kind of sign? I was about to find out. I was young and dumb, for sure.

We started dating and getting to know each other. He told me that he had broken up with his fiancée about three months earlier because she was abusive and controlling—I didn't know then that he was actually telling me things that *he* had done to her, but turning it around and telling me it was his fiancée. He also told me that he was really searching for God to help make him a better person. I offered him too much trust and too much grace because he seemed open and honest—even telling me of a situation where he had been violent towards his fiancée. I seem to offer too much trust too soon with a lot of people. I believed everything that he told me. He told me that he was a changed person. I reasoned that he must have changed; otherwise, why would he be telling me all this? He must have been telling the truth about changing because some of the things that he told me were bad. There were red flags for sure, but I believed him when he said he had changed. Like his telling me that he slammed his fiancée's head over and over again into a mattress when he was angry. There were other confessions about what he had done, but again, he said he was abused by his fiancée and trying to be a better person. So, I thought over everything that he had told me, and I decided that was then, and this was now, and he was better.

His dad was a worship leader. His mom made cookies for the church. He was the sound technician for their church. Their being members at their church aligned with my upbringing. I felt this was another sign that were meant to be together. We dated for three months and then he asked me to marry him. The red flags were there before he asked me to marry him. But I brushed all of them off. We are all flawed and need grace. I just didn't understand the difference between earnest improvement and a lie to make yourself look good.

I did not heed the warnings. We had been dating for about two weeks, and he was telling me that he was upset because he expected that when he called me, I should drop everything to be with him. I explained to him that I had chores to do. But it didn't matter. He would wait all day for me to call, and when I did call about five or six p.m. when all of my chores were done, he was angry. He said he was mad because he just wanted to spend time with me. His reaction just reinforced my thinking that he really loved me. He missed me. I wanted to make him happy, so I decided that I would give up some of the things I was doing even though they were important to me. Things like running and exercise. I decided that I would change my life and my schedule just to make him happy, and for a while, it did seem like we were both happy.

I had read a Christian book about qualities that you should look for in a spouse. I made a checklist of some of those qualities, and he had some of those qualities. He was tall, dark, and handsome, he had good values, he was kind to people, and he was a Christian. He checked off a lot of the boxes for good qualities when choosing a spouse.

Together, we planned our honeymoon and decided on a serene two weeks in a remote cabin. It was really all that we could afford. For whatever reason, the cabin owners had to cancel our reservation. Suddenly, this left us scrambling and without any honeymoon plans. My parents and extended family members, after hearing all this, and much to my surprise, graciously and generously paid for us to take a cruise for our honeymoon.

After my family shared this generous gesture and news with us, we headed home to our newly rented apartment, where he stayed while I still lived with my parents until our wedding day. As soon as we both walked inside the door, my soon-to-be husband threw himself on the floor and started weeping and wailing. He told me that the reason that he was so upset was because he believed that my family was trying to control his life. To say that I was stunned and in total disbelief is an understatement. I certainly did not see this generous gesture from his point of view at all. For me, I felt that this was a most beautiful, generous, and loving gift. So here I am, twenty-one years old, about to walk down the aisle to be married, and my soon-to-be husband has just had a meltdown over a gift from my family.

When we returned home to our apartment after our honeymoon, he became a totally different person. Before we were married, he wanted to spend every waking hour with me. After marriage, he chose not to spend any time together at all. Instead, he started spending all of his time with his best friend. He also started to shame me emotionally and verbally. He told me that he had married a broken person and that he had to try and fix me. We no longer spent any quality time together. He was gone almost all of the time, and he would shame me for being selfish if I verbalized being disappointed in his consistent absence.

He also started complaining that I was lazy and that I never did anything. I was confused as to why he would say this, and I was terribly hurt by the accusation because that simply was not true. It was not the case at all. I was feeling desperate to try and find a way to show him how much I was trying to be a good wife for him and how much I really did do. So, to show him how much I was accomplishing, I decided to make a spreadsheet detailing my daily, weekly, and monthly chores. And on top of all that, I was working a full-time job. When he saw the chart and how it proved how much I truly was accomplishing, instead of him saying, "Good job," he flipped it on me. He turned it all around.

He told me that I was just trying to make him look bad because I had more checkmarks on the spreadsheet than he did. That I was being disrespectful to him by trying to make myself look better. That was not my intention at all. I truly wanted to measure up and show him how hard I was trying. It never occurred to me, even once, to try and make myself look good and to make him look bad. I could not win. He constantly moved the goalposts on me, and there was nothing that I did or could do that was ever right. It was never enough. I felt it was probably never going to be good enough for him.

At twenty-six years old, I was pregnant with our first child, a daughter. After she was born, our precious baby daughter had stomach issues and was sick and crying most of the time. I was in and out of the pediatrician's office trying to get her better while he continued with his life as though our daughter didn't even exist. That is unless he could come off as the hero regarding an issue the baby was having, especially if other people were around to impress. One of my husband's bright remedies, because he was smarter than the doctors, was to break icicles from the roof and let her suck on them. He felt sucking on the cold ice would help her, never mind the dirty germs, dirt, and grit. she was digesting. He was always the smartest man in the room. And as for me, and as far as he was concerned, I knew absolutely nothing. I was hopeless and helpless.

I gave birth to our son about twenty-two months later. All the while I was pregnant, I suffered from terrible migraines and morning sickness. Unfortunately, I ended up losing my job because of it.

Our daughter was still sick when I gave birth to our son, so it was a very difficult time. Most of my time and energy was spent caring for both, just as it should have been. However, my husband did not feel the same way about that. One day, he presented me with a Christian book on how to be a good wife. This deeply hurt me. I was trying to do my very best. We had a sick toddler and a newborn, and he was never home and around to help me. *How is it*, I questioned, *that I am the one who needs to learn how to be a better spouse?*

It was hard for me to understand why the guy that I was married to was so different from the guy his friends and others knew and saw when he was with them. He was seen by them as a great guy. In fact, I have heard others say that he seems almost perfect, and he plays that role well. They sympathized with him for having such a terrible wife. He complained and talked about me to anyone and everyone. In fact, it has not stopped. It is still going on. Behind closed doors, he is a very different person from the one they think they know, and if they knew how poorly he speaks about them behind their backs, they might think twice.

It is hard for others to believe because he helps people with construction projects, works on their cars, and is always ready and willing when someone needs something. My husband was then and is now a malignant narcissist, and he used flying monkeys to discredit and hurt me. He told his friends and anyone who would listen that I was crazy, a horrible person, and a terrible wife and mother. I've lost so many people who I thought cared, loved me, and were my friends because of this.

"Flying monkeys" or "FMs" are the brainwashed minions that a narcissist uses to carry out their hurtful and hateful deeds and bidding, just like the Wicked Witch of the West in *The Wizard of Oz* and her faithful flying monkeys. It turns out that it is quite common for FMs to be recruited after a breakup to help with the gossip and smear campaigns. The whole plan is simple— to turn as many people against you as possible. There are no limits as to how far they will go. Mean and hateful lies are delicious, juicy gossip for the FMs.

I was defenseless against the attacks and lies.

He asked me for a divorce on New Year's Day in 2013. When

filing for divorce, he wanted to have complete control over that, too. He also demanded we file for bankruptcy because he didn't want to take any of my mistakes into his new life. I didn't even know what he meant, but he told me that if I didn't file with him, the creditors would all come after me. I was afraid, so I agreed. Now I know that I was only responsible for the debt of the mortgage. Somehow, my then-husband had managed to rack up roughly 85k worth of credit card debt, and my name wasn't on those cards. I didn't know he had been spending like that and shaming me simultaneously for going five dollars over our grocery budget. He said he wanted disillusionment and a 50–50 split, and he did not want the kids to impact his ability to live his life. The disillusionment was not fair to me and the kids, so I did not agree with it. I worked on filing for divorce with a lawyer of my own. The day he was served the papers, he came to the house, and he was angry. I had just been grocery shopping, and the groceries were sitting on the counter as I was about to begin putting them away. He pulled out his phone, and he started film-ing the groceries on the counter to try and prove that I was a slob and an unfit mother. I moved towards him to stop him, and then I grabbed his phone. He threw me hard against the wall three dif-ferent times as he screamed in my face for daring to file against him using "neglect and abandonment," which is legally required to indicate when filing in the state we live in. I saw his rage, and I knew I was in danger. I knew he intended to hurt me. I gave his phone back to him, and then I called the police. The police did make a report on the incident. The police reached out to him over the phone, and he agreed to bring the kids to the station for our exchange time that night. He went to the police station, and he filed a complaint against me. He told the police that I was lying. He told them that I had started the whole fight over money and that I had pushed him. By the time the prosecutor's office reached out to me, I asked them not to file charges for fear of retaliation. They did not bring charges.

By March 2014, our divorce was final. He had already started dating someone and moved in with her soon after the divorce was final. Our daughter was four, and our son was two. He had visitation with the kids on the weekends. Without fail, when they came home from their weekend with their dad, they always had rashes on their genitals and around their anus area. I was concerned, so every Monday after they returned from their dad's house, I would take them both to the doctor. The doctor would look at the rash and then prescribe treatment for it. It would start to clear up during their time with me, but after spending the weekend again with their father, when they came home, they had the rash in the same area again. The doctor diagnosed the rashes as suffering from staph infections and yeast infections, and this went on for several months.

Before we were divorced and still married, my ex-husband raped me several times. He liked having sex forcefully. He was always more aroused by being forceful and hearing me begging him to stop as he threw me against a wall or a dresser and tore my clothes off. That is how he liked sex the best. This was not lovemaking. So, knowing this about him and his sex addictions, I was worried about what my kids might possibly be subjected to. I worried about what could be happening on their weekends at their dad's. I needed advice. I needed to protect my children.

I talked to my attorney, and he told me that my pursuing this legally would most likely be hopeless, and the kids would be exposed to a lot through the whole process. He said the kids were so young, and a prosecutor would not be able to put them on the stand. He didn't give me much hope at all. Furthermore, he said that even if I could prove this issue, the court would likely not care.

So then, next, I asked our doctor to help me with a possible case. He referred us to a pediatric specialist. The exam they gave my daughter did not prove anything for sure because the hymen was still intact, but I was told many sexual abuses can happen without breaking the hymen and that the hymen can grow back as well. So, as it turns out, the timing for checking into a concern like this is critical. The only way to be sure would be to pay close attention to things she might say that seem unusual for her age.

Doctors and others were closely watching everything after visits with their dad, and eventually, the rashes cleared up.

In 2017, my ex sued for full custody. He told the court that all that I do is lay around the house and that I am a lazy and unfit mother. I tried to prove to the court that he had abusive behavior and that I feared for my kids.

This continues to be ongoing, with him dragging me into court and trying to prove that I am an unfit mother year after year. He does not help the kids with anything, so he is not doing this for any other reason than to mess with me. He knows that I will do without things that I need to give and provide for my kids. He is just trying to hurt me in every possible way that he can. Unfortunately, at the same time, it is deeply hurting our children. I am not afraid that he could prove me unfit because I know, and my kids know, that I am a good mother. A devoted and loving mother. But because he pays child support, he feels he's doing enough, even refusing to pay for things he's ordered to do so by the court, to pay for other needs that are outside of child support and that the system can't help me with.

My daughter came home during the summer of July 2021, and that was the very last time that she went to stay with her dad. It's now been two years.

My daughter started crying and having a meltdown in July that summer about having to go to her dad's. She was overly distraught and said that she was going to kill herself. Her father was on the phone at the time, and he backed down right away and said that it was okay, she did not have to come over. Her overall behavior around this time was changing, too. She was acting out and doing things that were not like her. One example of that was when she took $150.00 from my earnings without asking, which she had never done, and then she asked me if she could go to the store. I knew she had taken the money, and so I questioned her and asked her why. I asked her to please talk to me and tell me why she was suddenly acting this way.

She broke down and started crying, and told me that her dad had hurt her. She was pointing down on her body to where he hurt her. She could not say the words because she was so emotional. My boyfriend was close by in the room with us, and he heard and saw everything. She still could not bring herself to use the name of the body part she had pointed to. She was upset, emotional, and crying. I felt sick to my stomach, and I was angry. I could not fathom how he could do this to our daughter. I felt I had to call the police. I had to report this monster. When I spoke to the police, they said that the charge would have to be made in the county where it happened. I followed their orders and contacted the police there. After the report was filed, Child Protective Services became involved.

Everything that happened and was happening was scary. My precious daughter had something bad happen to her, and because of it, she was threatening to kill herself. We needed help. We were in a crisis.

I began to look for places to turn to. Her dad and I agreed she needed to see the therapist that she had previously seen for anxiety. These sessions revealed a real concern. The therapist believed my daughter was telling the truth.

The next step in the process was that we were referred to the CAC (Children's Advocacy Center) so that my daughter could be interviewed by the CPS (Child Protective Services) and a case-worker on video. As my daughter was being interviewed private-ly, I was handed documents to read. Those documents outlined how common these issues are in families, and so many more go unreported.

This nightmare journey has opened our eyes to the abuse that surrounds us. It happens to more victims than we ever really know or hear about. It is swept under the rug. I want to help not just my children, but I also want to help others.

My daughter and I, accompanied by the CPS agent, went to the doctor's office for the exam. My daughter understandably dreaded every bit of this. She cried during the exam while I stood by her side, and I held her hand. She turned her head and said that she hated me. I knew she didn't hate me; she hated having to go through this. She hated everything and everybody at that min-ute. The physical exam showed that the hymen was intact. But the doctor said that this is not the measure for full proof. He said the hymen can grow back. He said he was focusing more on the questions that he had asked her and the answers and descriptions that she told him. He said for him that was proof enough. He believed that something was going on, and he agreed to help pro-ceed with our case. The case worker informed us that she needed to consult with a supervisor about the case. She explained that we had waited too long before speaking up about this, and from her own prior experience in these types of cases, prosecutors are reluctant to even take the case.

Both of my kids, in one of the reports, had told the CPS worker that their dad had told them that it feels good to have a penis inside of a woman. The CPS worker defended their dad and said he was just trying to give them some sex education. The kids also had told her that they were afraid to go to their dad's. One would think this would be a red flag for child protection.

My ex was given a lie detector test, and he passed. He always touts that he is a man with integrity. In court, he always has a story that he has concocted that makes him look good and makes me look bad. A lie detector test doesn't tell you if someone is telling the truth. A lie detector test is only as good as the person reading the results, which is why it isn't admissible as evidence in court. It's too inaccurate and meant to only be an investigative tactic. The "passed" lie detector test was all that was needed to change the caseworker's months of investigation from Indicated (believed but not enough physical evidence to convict) to Unsubstantiated (not believed). One inaccurate test overturned months of the investigation.

It feels like the system is broken. I just want to protect my children.

Our next step was with the county ombudsman. She said her job was limited. She could only review all the evidence and make a recommendation to CPS, but she could not require them to follow her assessment. The ombudsman, after months of gathering files, evidence, etc., found that the original finding of Indicated was accurate, by law, and should be reinstated. However, CPS refused to change it back to Indicated.

It is like being in a maze of madness with lawyers and social services, therapists, police, county personnel, and doctors; it seems like it is all to beat you down until you just give up. Is there truly help out there? You start to wonder. But we must follow through for the sake of our children.

My ex is threatening me by appearing in places that I am at. Places he has never been, like my live performances. CPS had to talk to my daughter's school to inform them that their father was not allowed to pick my son up at any time, for any reason, nor to see him during the investigation for his safety. I arrive at school fifteen minutes early at the end of the school day for pick-up to avoid the risk. Regardless, my ex was there on the first day, filming me on his phone. How did he know I was going to be there early for pick up and on the *first* day this started?

I had to contact the domestic violence department because he started following me. I was granted an emergency CPO (Civil Protection Order), but the detective handling the investigation told me not to list my daughter's situation or the investigation into my ex, as he had not been informed, and they didn't want him tipped off. My ex violated that order and was arrested, but because he had no "paper trail" of offenses, he was released. This is still an ongoing fluid situation. I told CPS that I believed my ex needed therapy. I am still haunted by his perversions. His bestiality addiction while growing up on the dairy farm. His fantasies about raping.

Every fiber of my being knows my daughter is telling the truth. He has a history and thirst for sexual deviant behavior. His attraction to pornography, being loving towards me, and then flipping out and turning it into violent sex. The act of violently raping me was his way of lovemaking. So many red flags were there, and I did not pay attention to them. The many stories he told me before we were married about living on a dairy farm and his sexual acts on dairy animals. At the beginning of our relationship, I would always come back and say that he was a better person now with God. I believed him.

While I was pregnant with our son, our daughter would lie in her crib crying because of her stomach pain. We had been doctoring and changing the food she ate and her formulas, always trying to get to the bottom of what was making her sick. It was breaking my heart to hear her cry and feel sick all the time. Her dad would only get more agitated. One of those times, I said to him that he was not being a good dad because of the way he was acting. I explained to him that she could not help crying. For this, he flew into a rage, and it did not matter to him that I was pregnant at the time. He slammed my head against the wall so hard that I feared I might pass out.

Scared for my life, my unborn baby, and my daughter, I locked her and myself in the bedroom that night. That night, he slept on the couch. My locking that door to protect us and keep him away enraged him even more. The next morning, he threatened me that I had better never lock that door again.

In 2017 and 2018, we were assigned a guardian *ad litem* (GAL). My lawyer had to request that the GAL's report be dismissed because she had not completed all the requirements of the investigation to submit a report, as outlined by the State of Ohio. In 2021, we had a motion in court to protect my son and daughter. We asked to have a different GAL assigned so as not to have bias. After having her report dismissed for not telling the state-established guidelines, we were denied a new GAL and assigned the previous one. The GAL's first question to me in my portion of this interview was to recount in as much detail each time my husband had raped me. I was then asked if I ever said "no." I explained that at first, you always say no, but after years, you learn it ends quicker if you don't fight or say no. For my interview and my discussion about my husband raping me when we were married, as it turns out, and this is important for all you other victims, it is not considered rape if you don't say "no."

My son has a memory of being at his dad's house in a dark room, with the door closed and tied to a chair. He is eleven years old now, and he is still afraid of the dark. His father weaponized that fear.

Eventually, I had to give up CPO to protect myself and my son from the possibility of being separated. I was coerced into it by the GAL, an officer of the court. My heart breaks because my son is afraid to visit his dad. I fear for him. I also fear that I do not know everything. After going to his dad's, he comes home feeling sick. I feel like my house is on fire, and we are trying to escape while still alive.

My son is still visiting his dad, and he wants to have a relationship, but he says he does not feel like his dad really loves him. His dad has him spend time with his cousin instead of spending time with him. Before, when both kids visited their dad, he always favored him over his sister. Now, he hardly spends any time with him at all.

I recently realized something that I was not fully aware of in my ex-husband's behavior and actions. Whenever he starts being nice and acting as though he cares, I start to let my guard down. He draws me in, and I believe that he is coming from a good place, but he is actually laying a trap for me. It is a pattern, and it has taken me way too long to catch on to this.

My daughter says she wants to become a family court lawyer and a magistrate because she wants to save kids just like her and give them the justice that she did not get. She also wants to go to Harvard Law. Recently, she was gifted a new Doberman puppy. This is a wonderful gift for many reasons. One is that the puppy gives her something else to focus on and lovingly care for. She also feels the dog will protect her. She has had a fear, ever since she told us about her dad and what he did to her, that one day he might retaliate against her. She is terrified to be at home alone, so we make sure that never happens. When I am working, she stays with my parents. This new sense of security with the dog is making a very big, positive difference for her. It is a first line of defense for her.

I share this with others: try to stay strong and never give up hope. There are resources out there to turn to, even though the process and living through it is hard, and it doesn't always work. But keep trying.

For us, this is an ongoing and fluid situation. At the time of writing this, many things as they are now could change and even become worse.

Be careful who you choose to be with and who will be the co-parent of your children. It affects you and your children for the rest of your lives. I'm speaking for a man or a woman. Don't ignore the red flags in any relationship.

Have faith and courage as you fight to survive. The alternative is to give up and give in.

This fight is for our children, and they are worth it.

DON'T ASK ME WHY

Till the day that I die, I'm going to love that guy

Please don't ask me why all I'll do is cry

He has this power over me a key to my sanity

My heart is in his hands I wish I could understand

From the day that we met even now, I don't regret

I'm not angry, surprisingly

Yet, please don't ask me why I stayed, why I prayed, why I
obeyed

When I knew he had betrayed

Don't ask me why my love didn't fade

When my trust was gone don't ask me why I didn't move on

It took me years to realize I wasn't seen in his blue eyes

Don't ask me why I lived this lie or why I love this guy

One day after years of tears I faced all my fears

HEALING YOUR LIFE

Don't ask me why I finally asked this guy

If he still wanted me in his life if he still wanted me as his wife

He couldn't look me in the eyes and the Lord knows that I cried

I left him alone and I moved from our home

I no longer cry please don't ask me why

Bonnie A. Honaker

Chapter Sixteen:

In the End, His Life Truly Had Counted for Something. But He Had Struggled Throughout All His Life Thinking That He Didn't Matter

MEMORIES THAT WERE TOLD.

He always had a spark in his eyes, and he would weave back and forth when he spoke to you.

His smile was full of mischief, and his excitement when seeing you was real. His life hadn't always been easy for him. But he hadn't made life easy for so many others who were around him and knew him, either. And yet, on the day of the gathering for his "Celebration of Life," there seemed to be a loving acceptance of who he was despite it all. Even after all the dark places that he had been in and all the demons that he struggled with, on this day, all of that seemed to have peacefully faded away. As we watched the pictures about his life roll across the screen, we smiled, we cried, and we remembered the best of his life. This day belonged to him.

He was seventy-two years old on the day that he died. He was the father of two, one daughter and a son. His precious soul mate Mandy had died from cancer twelve years earlier.

At his Celebration of Life, the first pictures that rolled across the screen were his baby pictures. That brought back a memory for so many of us in the room who had heard him say so many times before that he never felt loved by his parents. Especially his mother. He always felt his mother resented her children, especially him, because she felt trapped having to stay at home to care for them. She wanted to travel the world, not be a homemaker and be tied down raising kids. He had one brother and a sister.

At a young age, he was diagnosed with ADHD, so he struggled in school, which added to his feelings of not being as smart as others and not ever quite measuring up. Not because this is true about having ADHD, but because that is what he understood it to mean. However, he did have a hot temper and mood swings, and both behaviors are associated with ADHD. This hot temper over the years caused him to lose a few friends and hurt others who were close to him.

"Buzz" was the nickname that he had adopted for himself in high school, and it stuck. He never liked his real name. His nickname, he thought, sounded a whole lot cooler. Mandy, his soul mate, was not his wife, and she was not the mother of his children. Buzz was two years older than Mandy, and they both had a big crush on each other. However, Mandy's parents did not approve of their age difference because Mandy was just a freshman in high school at the time they met, so she was not allowed to date him.

In high school, he wanted to be an athlete, so he decided to become a runner. He told the story that he knew that he was too skinny for football and he was not good at or built for much else, so this seemed to be his best and only choice to be able to say that he was an athlete.

He graduated in 1969. It has been said that the year 1969 left its mark in history as one of the most culturally defining years to date. This was the era of Woodstock, flower power, war demonstrations, and traveling to the moon on Apollo 11. Buzz was drafted to go into the military after his high school graduation. He would be serving and fighting for his country in the Vietnam War. His mandatory draft number had been called, along with several other of his buddies who also had low numbers in the draft, so they had to go. Sadly, not all of them survived the war to make it back home alive. Many of those who did make it home suffered injuries, PTSD, and other afflictions. They were never quite the same. One of his best friends was a tunnel rat. As told in an article titled "Vietnam Vermin: The Story of The Tunnel Rats," published in March 2019, shares that at the time of Operation Crimp, these tunnel complexes included hospitals, storage facilities, barracks, training areas, and the Viet Cong headquarters, running from Saigon down to the Cambodian border. This network of tunnels was so extensive that it was believed by some to be capable of holding up to 5,000 Viet Cong for several months.

The bravery of the men fighting against the Viet Cong who

were chosen to be tunnel rats is beyond any understanding of how they ever survived it. The tunnels were so small and tight that it required a smaller man of five feet six inches or less to be able to move around in the small space inside the tunnel. It also required strong courage to even go down into the tunnel because you knew your chances of coming out were not good.

The tunnels had booby traps, grenades, and punji sticks. There were poisonous snakes, scorpions, rats, bats, and more. When you came face to face in the tunnel with the enemy, you needed to try and kill them before they killed you, all while you were stuck in a tiny dark space. If you used your gun, the echo of the shot was deafening, and then it alerted more of the enemies and more danger.

He always had a special admiration for his brave friend, who was a tunnel rat. He also spoke highly of all the other guys he knew who served their time bravely, saw and lived through some terrible things, and were able to make it back home.

Buzz made it through boot camp, but he was then released because he was deaf in one ear. They gave him a medical deferment. He could have been a liability to himself and others in combat. This was a mixed bag of emotions for him. He was spared from being sent to the front lines, but his heart ached for his buddies who had to go. He felt survival guilt and relief at the same time. War is raw and ugly and leaves wounds and scars that never heal.

Buzz was still passionate about running. He competed more than once in the Boston Marathon, and he had good finishes each time. He ran numerous other competitions, and he won numerous awards. He loved it because he was good at it, and competing and winning made him feel better about himself. He took pride in himself. It felt good. His trophies, medals, and pictures were displayed in many of the rooms in his house.

This part of the story cannot be confirmed for sure. But it was told by others that on the day that Buzz was at the altar marrying his first wife, Mandy sat in a pew at the back of the church with tears running down her face. Thinking about this story and this day seems like a scene right out of a movie. Mandy also ended up marrying someone else, who was eleven years older than her. Together, they had a daughter. But Mandy and Buzz's flame never extinguished. When both of their marriages ended years later, they found each other again and picked up right where they had left off so many years before.

Buzz's not feeling loved as a child was something that he never got over. He didn't understand how his mother could have felt that way about him because, as a parent himself, he absolutely adored and loved his kids. Through all the years, even the years that his kids lived miles away after his divorce, his eyes would always light up whenever he spoke of them. His long-time neighbors and friends who lived next door shared that he loved spending time with his kids. They said that he was always doing something fun with them, along with Mandy.

He carried the hurt of not feeling loved as a child with him throughout his entire life. He could never shake the feeling that he was unworthy and unwanted. No matter how fast he ran or how many times he won the race, he never felt deserving of any of it. He thought he would just have to keep running until he did. He would run until he could feel deserving and better about himself and who he was.

Buzz was in two bad car accidents, but it was a terrible motorcycle accident that impacted the rest of his life. It is said that it was a miracle that he even survived. He never fully recovered from it. During this time, he was treated with some strong opioids to ease the immense pain he was in. The drugs caused him to suffer a drug addiction that he had to battle with, and he sought treatment for it.

After the motorcycle accident, he decided to be baptized, and he started going to church. He knew that he had almost died in that accident, and he felt God had spared him. He felt God had something more in store for him. He had been told by his doctors they were surprised he survived. This was when Mandy came back into his life. He was an alcoholic at the time, but he agreed to go through treatment for help before Mandy would agree to their getting back together.

He was dedicated to beginning to live a better life. A life without drugs and alcohol. A life with Mandy and God. Mandy was his trophy. She made him feel deserving. He knew she deserved the best. She was loved by her students, faculty, friends, and family. She was somebody very special. She lit up the room with her smile. His mother didn't love him, but Mandy did.

Many of her friends did not like Buzz. They knew that he had addictions. They thought Mandy deserved more and someone better in her life. But the two of them had something special between them. It was a genuine love for each other.

They had eight good years together before Mandy became sick. He started drinking again. He was struggling to cope. He knew she was dying. He wanted it to be him, not her. Before she died, she asked her sister to please watch over him. Her sister had already left her teaching job to move in to help take care of Mandy. Her sister promised that, yes, she would watch over him. Little did she know that this would be a monumental commitment. After Mandy died, Buzz's world began to crumble. Once again, he turned to drugs and alcohol to ease the pain. He became very dependent on Mandy's sister. The years that followed were hard.

His faithful dog, Sully, was given to him by Mandy. He was a rescue dog who won both of their hearts immediately. All through their years together, Sully brought them so much joy and companionship! During Mandy's illness, Sully was supporting them both. After Mandy's passing, Sully became an even stronger pillar of strength for Buzz. He always believed that

Mandy adopted Sully for him to have after she was gone. They did everything together; Sully meant the world to him!

At the age of fourteen, Sully became weaker, and Buzz knew

it wouldn't be long before Sully would leave him, too. The day it happened, he was devastated. He lived three months without Sully and grieved his loss every single day as he had grieved Mandy's.

He was all alone and trying to figure out what this chapter of his life was supposed to look like. He started thinking about selling their home. He could no longer drive because of the head trauma that he had suffered years before from the accident. He said he felt isolated living there because you really needed to be able to drive so you could get to a grocery store and restaurants. He started thinking about selling the house and moving to the small town near where he grew up. He had friends there, and he could walk to the nearby stores. But this was a hard decision for him to make. No matter how much sense it might have made, he did not want to move and leave behind his memories of Mandy and Sully and their time living together in their home.

For someone who had lived such a hard and troubling life, it seemed so unfair that he would have died such a tragic death. It was a bright and warm sunny day when he was visiting his neighbor who lived across the street from him. As he left their house and was walking back across the street to his home, he was hit and killed by a hit-and-run driver. The impact was so bad that he was thrown into the air before hitting the ground several yards away at the corner of the street that he lived on. It was several months before the police finally made an arrest.

Buzz sought help throughout his life for guidance and

strength to help him deal with his life's choices, decisions, and hurdles. He struggled to be happy, which is all he ever wanted. He didn't grow up knowing God's unconditional love; as an adult, he had glimpses of it, but it wasn't deep enough to anchor him. Buzz's feelings of inferiority overwhelmed him at times, which took him down the roads he never intended to go. All of us who knew and loved him along the way tried to help him see his self-worth and that he mattered and was valued. We tried to support him as best we could, but there comes a time when you have to step away, let go, and let God. If only he could have known how much he was loved.

Being hit by a speeding car while walking home from a neighbor's house across the street was a horrible way to leave this world. We all hoped and prayed that he did not feel any pain because the impact of that speeding car was gruesome. He had already suffered so much pain in his life. He didn't deserve this. So, from where we started this story, we will end it now with a focus on the guy who loved deeply and who touched many lives. Through all the tragedies that he suffered, he never gave up, even though some days were gut-wrenching and he thought otherwise. He was a runner, and many times, he was also a winner. Many times, he fell down, but at least he tried, and he got back up; he was not a loser. And his life did mean something to so many people, as we heard and saw on the day of his Celebration of Life. He can be at peace now, knowing that he did matter.

Sully was Buzz's final tangible gift from Mandy. His ashes

were mixed with Buzz's ashes after he died.

They were buried together at Mandy's grave.

Chapter Seventeen:

I Need a Magic Eraser to Erase the Awful Trauma That Continues to Haunt My Life

CINDY'S INTERVIEW AND STORY.

One of my biggest struggles is coming to grips and being able to understand why my mother let her kids suffer the way that we did for our entire childhood. She told us her reasons, and she gave us lots of explanations before she died. But even now, more than fifty years later, her many reasons all fall short and completely fail all understanding at all levels.

She was my mother, and I loved her. But that does not mean I can't be sad, hurt, broken and honest about the decisions and choices that she made. The choices that constantly put all our lives at times in great danger and caused us immense suffering.

My mother, siblings, and I all suffered greatly. But the story I want to share is not about all of them. This is my chapter, my story, and my chance to speak out on paper in the hopes that I might release more of what I have kept bottled up inside of me. To let go of more of the hurt and pain that I carry around with me every day. I go to sleep thinking about it, and I wake up thinking about it. Many times, I wake up during the night gasping and trying to catch my breath and shaking because I am terrified that he is coming for me. It takes me hours to calm myself back down, and then I start to fear that if I fall back asleep, I might have the same nightmare all over again. The "he" that I am referring to is my stepfather. He continues to haunt my life, even from his grave.

My reasons for doing this are not for any selfish reasons or for hoping others will have pity on me. I have had years and years of therapy, and so I have already done a lot of talking and crying. I have been prescribed, over the years, to take lots of different medications for anxiety, depression, and PTSD. The drugs help to numb you a bit, but the gnawing and sadness never go away. I used alcohol to mask the pain and how I felt about myself. There were times I used illegal drugs, hoping they would be a magic cure for my life. So, I look at this opportunity as another kind of therapy by committing to paper some of my life story. This feels a little different. It feels like I can open up a little bit more about my life. It feels a little safer. My purpose for doing so is pure. I not only want to help myself, but I also want to give hope to others. I don't have to use my real name, and I don't have to know yours. Our identities are not what is most important. We just need to know that we are broken. We know what that feels like, but we are not without hope. Each day is a fresh start, and I feel good about myself, knowing that I am a better mother, grandmother, and person. What I hope and pray for the most is to be compassionate and caring toward others. To do better and be better. It is rocket fuel for my soul.

Unfortunately, because I was the youngest, I was the last child to leave home. It was just me and my mother left in the house to suffer the brunt of the physical, sexual, and emotional abuse from my stepfather. The only ones left for him to torture. He was my mother's second horribly bad decision in her choice of husbands. Her first bad choice for a husband was my father. He was a drunk and a womanizer who was gone for weeks at a time. He was never around very much at all. Just long enough to come home drunk and to get my mother pregnant again. Seven times, seven children.

Every day growing up with my stepfather, I heard how stupid I was and how I would never amount to anything. You hear it so much that you own it. You believe it. It sticks to you like glue. Your self-confidence is mostly nonexistent, so you feel diminished and inadequate. You have low expectations for your life. You feel undeserving. This low, diminished feeling you have of yourself reinforces the path and choices that you make. I have never felt strong enough to believe that I deserved or could have very much in my life.

I do know what it is like to do without. To feel poor and to be poor. As the youngest child, I got all the "hand-me-downs." I wore shoes that did not fit, socks that did not match, clothes that were too big and tattered and soiled. Presents and gifts were scarce around our house, and when I try to think of a special toy that I might have been given or had, nothing comes to mind.

I can't stand to see a child spanked or slapped out in public.

I remember so well being that child and having nowhere to turn for help. We were threatened to keep our mouths shut and not to speak in public. We were to remain silent even if asked any questions. My mother was not allowed to talk with anyone either. If she forgot and took part in a conversation, she was beaten when they returned back home.

One time, when my mother and stepfather went to the doctor's office for an appointment for him, he distracted the nurse at the checkout area. This was pre-planned. He had instructed my mother ahead of time that while they were there, she needed to steal the prescription pads that were kept at the front desk. He was on painkillers, and this would give him an endless supply. This not only provided him with the ability to obtain more drugs at different drug stores, but it was also a threat he held over my mother's head. He said she would be thrown into prison if he told the police about her stealing the prescription pads. Not only did she steal them, but he made her write out the prescription in her handwriting for the drugs that he wanted, and then she also had to go to the pharmacy and pick them up. This mastermind plan kept him innocent in all of it. She stayed obedient because this was just one of the threats that hung over her head.

One beating that I suffered from him was so severe that I could not sit down on my seat on the bus. I had to stand and hold onto the bars to keep from falling. I wore a dress to school that day because I could not bear to have pants on. The pants would rub against the bloody belt lashes I had on my back, legs, and buttocks. I also could not sit in my chair at school. Two of my friends had seen belt lash marks, bruises, and a lot more on me so many times before, but this time, they both agreed that this beating had gone way too far. They decided that they would report this beating and my condition to the teacher, who then, in turn, reported it to the authorities. My friends told me that they had to do something because they were sure that my stepdad was trying to kill me once and for all. They meant well, but I knew this was not going to end well for me. When my mother and stepfather found out that the authorities were coming to our house, all hell broke loose. I was told when the authorities showed up that if I told the truth about what had happened, that everyone in the house would suffer for it. My stepfather said that one at a time, each of my siblings would be beaten, and then my mother. And I shouldn't think for one minute that this would be all that there was to it. He told me that I would be beaten again, and this time, it would be worse than the last. He said my story would be that I had fallen down the stairs. I was to say that nothing bad had happened to me. It was just another one of my clumsy accidents. So, you see, our situation in our home, living with him, was hopeless. No help was ever going to come for us. There was no escape. For all the times that you wished and hoped that someone was coming to save you, time and time again, all hope was lost. It was never ever going to happen.

I became pregnant at the age of seventeen. My stepfather beat me until he was sure I would miscarry. He couldn't risk anyone thinking that it might possibly be his baby. And I did lose the baby.

After living through the terror of my horrible childhood, one would hope that once I was away from all that misery and had escaped, things in my life might be better. But it was not meant to be for me. And trust me, I asked God, "Why?" repeatedly.

After I was married, my husband's elderly father came to live with us. At the time that he moved in with us, he was suffering from PTSD. He was in the military during war times and had fought in some major battles. He was in his eighties, and his mental state was not at all good. My husband had asked me to please make a doctor's appointment for his dad. I was returning home from a trip, and I told him that I would take care of it as soon as I returned home. My father-in-law had been exhibiting unusual behavior for some time. Like bathing in the creek outside and washing his hair in the cold muddy water instead of using the bath inside of our house. I wondered if he thought he was still on the battlefield. On one particular day, my husband's sisters were over visiting with my husband, their dad, and myself. Suddenly, and out of nowhere, as we were all sitting in the living room, my father-in-law stood up and pointed his finger at me. He started yelling that I had raped him. He went on to say that I liked raping old men. He then accused me of raping my stepfather, who he had known for many years. He kept going on and on and said that he could prove that I had raped him because he saw my naked body. He went on and started describing where on my body I had scars and moles. He was pointing and yelling, and everyone was confused and scared by all this. He wouldn't stop his ranting, and he insisted that I strip down and show everyone in the room the scars and moles on my body. This would prove to everyone that I had raped him. I was in total shock, trembling and crying, and I motioned for the sisters to go into the bathroom with me, and I would prove to them I had none of the scars and moles on my body that he was describing. I stripped my clothes off, and they could see none of what he was describing and saying was true. Just the thought of him saying that I had raped my stepfather was horrifying to me. It threw me over the edge. I had been sexually abused and violently beaten by my stepfather since I was just four years old. And it didn't stop until I was well past the age of eighteen. How could he possibly be saying all this to me and about me? *Haven't I suffered enough in my life?* I thought. *Why is this happening?* I could not make sense of any of it.

We got things calmed down, and I tried my best to be understanding. I reasoned it out the best that I could and said to myself that he was not in his right mind and he was just terribly confused. Two days later, in the early morning, I asked him, trying to keep things as normal as possible, what he would like me to cook for him for breakfast. I wanted things to be better and calmer. I made him his breakfast that day: two sausage links, eggs, and fried potatoes. While he was sitting down at the table and eating, I told him that I was going outside for a little while to clean my storage building. I said I would be back then to check on him and see if he needed anything. After a few hours, I decided I would go back in the house and see how he was doing. I reached the back door of the house, and when I opened the door, my father-in-law was sitting on the floor looking directly at me, and he had a turkey rifle aimed at himself. I remember being shocked, and I asked him if he was okay, and that is when the gun discharged. The force of the blast, because of being at such close range, blew his head completely off. The sight of his horrible death has left for me a nightmare image that I cannot erase from my mind. To this day, we live in the same house, but there are no blinds or curtains on that back door. I must be able to see inside before opening my door. I must make sure nothing horrible is going to happen when I go through the door. I do not have blinds anywhere in my house. I can see in, and I can see out. In my living room, where he was sitting and waiting, I can't even go in there. Nothing has changed in that room, and it was twenty-six years ago.

The law enforcement team that responded to the call and that came to our house that day to investigate said that his suicide plan was one of the best-planned suicides they had ever seen. I often think how life must be awfully hard for first responders and all the horrors that they must see. They said that my father-in-law had taken his shoe off and had his toe on the trigger with the gun pointed directly at his head. He was ready and waiting for me as soon as I opened the door.

I left our house for close to a month. I could not stay there. The day that I finally came home, my husband held me, and I cried for hours. This day and the tragic memory of him killing himself still haunts me. My real father had also died just a month before this happened. But thankfully, my husband has been a tower of strength for me and has been at my side now for forty-five years. There is a dogwood tree that his father planted in our front yard. I try to hold on to this to have a good memory of him instead of the horror I remember and witnessed on the day he died.

Unfortunately, I was not a good student. The only two subjects that I was any good at were math and home economics. Reading, English, spelling, and writing are all subjects I failed terribly at.

Even my grandparents were not supportive of me. Always comparing me to my siblings or others. I never measured up, and neither did my husband. When I asked my mother before she died why she made the choices that she did and kept us in the abusive nightmare that we lived in, her answer was only to say that one day I would understand. She said that what she thought was most important for us was being able to keep us all together. I am not so sure. It is like being together on a sinking ship. We were together, but together, we were all going down. We all have scars, nightmares, trauma, and depression. I'm not sure about finding the good in all that, but I do know I love my siblings. And I am deeply sad that all of us lived such a terrible childhood.

I am still working on more healing. I don't think you can ever say you are healed. The life that I endured can't be changed, and it can't be fixed. There is no cure. I carried these words with me most of my life: "God don't make no junk." It helped me to know, at least in God's eyes, I had worth.

I do believe that I am a window of hope for others because I know so very well what hell looks like and feels like, so I genuinely care and have compassion for others who are suffering.

I find beauty and love in caring for plants. I enjoy working in greenhouses. I have worked in a couple of different greenhouses for over the past fifteen years. Sometimes, I will meet someone who I think needs a smile or a kind word. I have more peace within myself here. I love planting seeds and then watching them grow. I nurture the seeds, water them, and let the sun shine over them. It makes me feel that I am good at something. I am good at this. And a tiny seed symbolizes for me new beginnings. Fresh starts. It gives me hope. It makes me smile.

I wish for others fresh starts, hope, and more reasons to smile.

Chapter Eighteen:

Bad Decisions Have Consequences. What Do You Do When Bad Decisions Made by Others Affect Your Destiny?

REX'S INTERVIEW AND STORY.

We had been married for about a year when we decided it would be a good time in our life to start our family. We both had good jobs and a nice house with a fenced-in backyard. It would be perfect, we thought, for a sandbox, a swing set, and the children we planned to have. We wanted to start our family.

After two years of trying to get pregnant, sadly, we never had a positive pregnancy result. We were disappointed, but we were not without hope. After discussing what our options might be with our doctor, our next possibility was to try IVF, *in vitro* fertilization. The success rates for this vary in a wide percentage range. We were told that the range is anywhere between twelve to seventy percent. But along with factoring in the success rate, you also need to take into consideration another big factor, which is the high cost of the treatment. The cost for IVF ranges between fifteen thousand and twenty-five thousand dollars. That is a lot of money for a lot of people. And it is not covered by insurance. Another big factor that hopeful parents must know about at the onset is that there is a chance of having twins or multiple births. Both of us are from large, loving families, so having children and a family was something we had always hoped, prayed for, and dreamed of. It didn't matter if it was one baby, twins, or even more. We did not hesitate to give our answer. We told the doctor to *sign us up*. We had made the decision, and we were anxious about moving forward. We were both filled with anticipation and excitement when we left the doctor's office that day.

Our first round of implanting the eggs did not work. We knew there was a possibility of this happening, but we were still deeply disappointed. We knew that this IVF attempt that failed meant that we had to make another decision. That decision would be about trying again. Our trying again would mean taking more money out of our savings. But this really wasn't a hard decision for us, because we really wanted a baby. We discussed it, and we both strongly felt that we wanted to try this procedure a second time. We were extremely happy when the second round was successful. We were on cloud nine and on top of the world. But when Sandy was about twelve weeks pregnant, sadly, we lost our baby. Sandy had suffered a miscarriage, and we were both heartbroken. Our two hopeful attempts to have a baby had used up what money we had available. We simply could not afford to try and pay for a third time. We had given up a lot to be able to afford to pay for the two IVF attempts. But regardless of the cost of the procedures and what we had to give up, we were still happy that we had gone forward and at least tried. Because the one thing that never changed for us was that we wanted to have children, be parents, and raise our family. We love children.

Along the way, we were approached by someone who told us that she had a grandson who was in the foster care system. She said the biological mother would not be getting him back, and so he would be eligible for adoption. Adoption sounded like an answer to our hopes of becoming parents. We contacted child services in the county where we lived and started making all the inquiries. Initially, we would be starting in the system first as foster parents. This would open the door for us and for the possibility of becoming adoptive parents.

The process to qualify to be foster parents is an extensive process, as it should be. We did not hesitate, and we did it all. We did all the background checks, medical exams, financial information, fire inspection, home inspection and home study, training, character references, and more. Even our pets had to have up-to-date vaccinations, veterinary exams, and licenses. Quite a thorough process, as one would hope it would be for the protection of the children.

Finally, we were told that we had qualified and that we had been approved to become foster parents. We were very excited and hopeful about having a child to love and care for. This was an answer to our prayers. During the process, for whatever reason, even though we had our hopes of being able to adopt the little boy that the grandmother had hoped we could adopt, it ended up that we were not able to.

We were in the system, so we just had to wait. When we got the call for our second child placement, we were very excited because it was a newborn baby boy. Sadly, his mother was a drug addict. She tested positive for every possible drug. There were traces of fentanyl, meth, cocaine, and heroin that were all in this little baby's system. He was placed in the NICU ward. The NICU ward is a neonatal intensive care unit, also known as an intensive care nursery. This intensive care unit (ICU) specializes in the care of ill or premature newborn infants. This poor little guy had a lot to suffer through being born addicted to all these drugs that his mother had been using. He was also born a month prematurely. Once we got the call that we would be fostering him, we immediately committed to do everything that we could to get him through all this. We were both at the hospital every night, helping to hold him and care for him. This also helped the staff out, too, as they had many other critical-care newborns that they had to care for. We wanted our little guy to know that he was safe and that he was loved. Day after day, we watched him twitch and struggle, and we held him close to comfort him. We had already fallen in love with him. We had been told that we would have a chance to adopt him. This is what we had hoped for. His mother had given him his name at birth. His name was Jacob. He was a beautiful baby boy with perfect little features and a lot of dark hair.

About three weeks after he was born, we were able to take

him home. We were so excited and had been looking forward to this day. The nursery in our home was filled with just about anything you might think of that one would want to have for a newborn baby. We can't express enough how excited and thrilled we were to be bringing this little bundle of joy into our home. And our families were very excited as well. This little guy would have a lot of love and support. This was so important to us that we would be giving a wonderful, loving home, a large, loving family, and a better life for this little guy. This is what the foster and adoption program strives for. We were going to give our very best. We were so happy and grateful.

Jacob's mother, we were told, would be allowed to visit him, but she would have to take a drug test prior to setting up her visit. The visit would also be supervised. Over the next six months, she only visited him one time.

During this time, we had Jacob at numerous pediatric appointments and scheduled therapy. A special agency called Help Me Grow was assigned to visit with us and Jacob and monitor his surroundings and his development. He was thriving, and all this was recorded and documented. He did have RSV, a respiratory virus, at one point and had to be treated. This was caused, we were told, because of the drugs his mother had used. He was given excellent medical care and recovered. If we had to take off work to get him to an appointment, we did. His care and needs were always what was most important.

We decided to buy a new house just so that we could be

closer to the daycare he would be attending, which was close to where Sandy worked. We wanted him close by and in a highly-rated daycare while we were working. He had suffered and survived so much because of his mother's drug addiction. We wanted him to have the best possible quality of life, one that was filled with lots of love.

One day, we got a call from CSB, Child Services Bureau, and they told us that they were moving the real mother out of the case management plan. This was around Thanksgiving. Shortly after that, we were contacted again, and we were told that a family member was requesting to have a visit with Jacob. CSB had cleared her. We were all new to this and the proper procedures, and so we followed through with what we were told. A caseworker with CSB, the family member, and both of us were all together on a Facetime call to talk about setting up a time for this visit. The family member, we were told, was a second cousin and was related to the baby's real father. The second cousin said that she was a nurse and, on the Facetime call that day, she did seem to be a nice person. She said that she lived a couple hundred miles north of us, so this meet-up would have to be scheduled over a weekend. We made plans for each of us to drive half the distance for the visit to drop Jacob off. We were already feeling sad, knowing it would be three long days without him. We were sad that we had to do this. But it was for Jacob's family. Jacob had not been away from us overnight since we had brought him home. We knew this was going to be hard.

I suggested that we meet at a family restaurant. Instead, the cousin chose to meet somewhere else, and she gave us the address. I put it in my GPS, and we were on our way.

The second cousin had three kids, and her husband came with her, too. The address that she had given to us to meet her at turned out to be at a bar. I did not know this until my GPS had us pulling into the parking lot. Immediately, something just did not seem right. We felt uncomfortable, and we couldn't shake that feeling. We left our little Jacob, along with everything possible we thought our little guy might need. We also left our cell phone numbers with her and said to please call us if she needed anything. No matter what time it was. We were both in tears all the way home. It would be the longest weekend of our life, we thought. We wondered how we would get through it. We kept reminding ourselves that we had been told that we would be able to adopt him, so once that was complete, we thought we would never ever have to do something like this again. Hopefully, this was a one-time-only deal.

We arrived back home, and the next morning, we received a text from the cousin. The text said, "Did anyone ever say anything about this bump on Jacob's back?" Shocked, we replied, "No, never." We had taken him to the pediatrician just two days prior, and the doctor was very pleased with his progress. I said as much to her. Thank God my sister-in law, who had worked for CSB in the past in another county, had advised us to take photographs of Jacob before we dropped him off. We followed her advice, so we had photos of him front and back, with the day and time that they were taken. The photos did not show any bump or even a mark on his back.

After we hung up the phone with her, Sandy and I were discussing the fact that she was a nurse. We tried to console ourselves that if this was bad enough, certainly she would take our little guy to the emergency room. She had medical training, after all. She would do the best thing for him. *Again*, we thought, *we just need to calm down; again, she is a nurse.*

The weekend was almost over, and the second cousin called us and told us that we could pick up Jacob. And this time she chose for us to meet her at a Walmart store. I anxiously made the drive to get our little guy. Sandy had to work. After I picked him up and I was driving home, little Jacob was in his car seat and he was acting fussy. He was fussy for the entire drive back to our house. Something didn't seem right with him. At the time I thought it might be because he wanted Sandy. He always responded better to her mothering and cuddling him. Once I was home with Jacob, we both thought that he sounded hoarse, like he had been crying for a long time. Sadly, we thought maybe he had been crying for the whole weekend. Sandy tried everything, and she could not get him to calm down, which was unusual.

We already had an appointment with the NIC unit. We also emailed our caseworker right away to inform them about the full and complete details of what took place. We documented from the time that we dropped him off to the time that I picked him up. We also took pictures of what he looked like after we got him home. Not only was there a bump on his back, but he also had a rug burn on his arm and a bruise on his forehead. None of these marks and bumps were there when we dropped him off. We had before and after pictures as proof. We were worried sick about what might have happened to our little guy.

We were in the process of moving to our new house, so we asked my dad to watch Jacob for us for just a little while. When we returned later to pick him up, my dad made the statement that he also thought that Jacob did not seem right either. My dad said that he was not rolling over like he had been before. My dad also said that Jacob did not want him to hold his arms and hands up so that he could try to take those little steps that he laughed and smiled about whenever he did this.

The time came for us to take Jacob for the appointment at the NICU and to try to get to the bottom of everything. They first took X-rays and a CT scan. I laid myself down on the table alongside him to help comfort him while they took the X-rays. The results showed that Jacob had suffered several broken bones in his back. None of which, thank God, were life-threatening, but nonetheless, this poor little guy had broken bones. They said it looked like he had been in a bad car accident. The staff next called in an emergency CSB team to further investigate and take the situation and matter over. Devastatingly, that day was the last time that we saw Jacob. We certainly never ever in a million years expected that. We thought that he would be treated, and he would heal, and we would be by his side through all of it. But that is not at all how any of it was handled. His injuries became an open investigation into what had happened to him.

We were shocked, hurt, and scared. We discussed this with our family, and we decided to hire an attorney. The attorney said that he wanted to get out in front of this, and so along with him collecting from us all our communications, calls, texts, photographs, and doctor appointments, he also had us take a lie detector test. The test results showed that we were innocent. We had no idea how he was hurt. The pediatrician and The Help Me Grow Therapy specialist who came to our house for visits both wanted to write letters about the wonderful care that we had given to Jacob. We also had many people who wrote letters of good reference for us.

CSB sent an investigator for the agency out to our house to question us. We were shocked that he did not want to see any of the before and after photos that we had taken, which would prove we were telling the truth and that we had done nothing wrong. The whole nightmare got even worse after we contacted the sheriff's department, the sheriff in the county for which the second cousin/nurse said that she lived. Well, that turned out to be a lie. She did not live there. She actually lived more than an hour and a half from there. Why did she lie about where she lived? Upon further investigation, it was also found out that she was not a nurse, and the real father of Jacob was related to the phony nurse. He was a first cousin to her.

We were told that CSB wanted to pin this on us but that they did not have enough proof. They said they would drop all charges against us but that we could no longer be foster parents in their county. However, we could be foster parents in another county if we chose to do so. It didn't make sense that this would be the outcome.

In conclusion, when you look at all this, the facts are that CSB approved the cousin by using or not using whatever as a background check. If they had done a background check, it would have proved she was not a nurse. The person they approved of was not only not a nurse, but she did not live where she said that she did. And so, where did she take Jacob that weekend, and what had happened to him? We do not know what steps CSB takes to verify people. But in this case, the facts were something drastically different. Before the visit and drop-off, CSB made a Facetime call with the cousin and with us to be able to set that meeting up. We were instructed to follow through with the drop-off. We followed CSB's instructions. Our pictures, doctor appointments, and detailed paperwork documented and proved that we dropped off a healthy baby boy to the cousin. A healthy baby was dropped off at a bar where the cousin, who was not really a nurse and had lied to CSB and us and said that she was, chose to meet. CSB perhaps did not want the photos, doctor reports, and conversations as proof in this matter because it would have made them liable for not properly vetting someone. Someone whom they permitted, arranged, and allowed to take Jacob. They arranged it and approved it. Whatever their vetting process is for setting up a visitation, we do not know. We do know that we certainly had to go through a lot to be properly vetted. We had background checks, inspections of our home, and more.

We were not comfortable with the drop-off from the start, but we had no right to tell them no. We have also been told that CSB typically favors the requests of family members. Blood relatives.

The foster care system has major failures. The system failed Jacob, and he was left unprotected and suffered injuries because of it. He suffered something terrible that weekend. And for that, we will forever be heartbroken. This little guy had such a horrible beginning in his life. The baby that we cuddled and loved every day, from the very first day that they called us and told us that they had a baby boy for us. They said it was a baby that you will most likely be able to adopt. The system tore a hole in our hearts that cannot be mended. Jacob stole our hearts, and they took him from us, and we had done nothing wrong. We loved him, protected him, and catered to and provided for him all his needs.

We have decided that we can't trust trying again. There is no way we would survive another loss or the possibility of a child being taken away.

Our hope, prayer, and purpose in sharing our story is to bring awareness to others. Something like this is too important to get wrong. A child's life was put in danger. A child that all we ever wanted for him was to love him, spoil him, and make him happy.

We pray each and every day for our special little guy, Jacob, and we hope and pray that he is healthy and safe.

Bad decisions have bad consequences.

CHAPTER NINETEEN:

IF ONLY I HAD BELIEVED WHAT ALL SHE WAS TELLING ME, I THINK IT IS POSSIBLE I COULD HAVE SAVED HER LIFE.

CHRISTINA'S INTERVIEW AND STORY.

Betsy and I became close friends in the seventh grade. Betsy lived with her grandmother in an old farmhouse that was just outside of the small town where I lived.

We did not go to grade school together because of the school boundary lines. So, the very first time that we met was when we started junior high. We met on the school bus on the very first day that we started junior high. I had already boarded the bus and was seated when the bus driver stopped in front of her house. This petite and pretty girl, with these big blue eyes, climbed the stairs of the bus and began looking around to find an empty seat. Something said to me to raise my arm and motion to her because there was a seat open right next to me. She saw my smile and my arm waving in the air, and she smiled back and then walked back to where I was sitting. It was seat number seventeen on the bus, and we were starting seventh grade. We both thought it was meant to be because we met at seven-thirty in the morning on September 7. From that very day going forward, we kept the details about our meeting as being special and significant just for us. We were both believers that there are no coincidences. The number *seven* from that day forward would be our lucky number.

Betsy was quiet and not very outgoing, but she was smart, and she was a lot of fun. I, on the other hand, had lots of brothers and sisters, so I wasn't a bit shy. My older siblings had told me how important seventh grade was because you had to establish yourself early on if you wanted to be popular. Three elementary schools merged their students for seventh grade. You had a lot of competition to compete with to be able to even be noticed. Especially if you wanted to take part in any extracurricular activities or if you wanted to try out for cheerleading, the dance team, or drama.

Betsy lived with her grandmother because her mother and father had been killed in a car-and-train accident when she was just five years old. Her grandmother worked at the nearby university as a law professor. Betsy resembled her grandmother in looks, and they had a very warm and loving relationship. But her grandmother was also a bit strict with her and who she was allowed to hang out with. I am pretty sure she probably had me checked out, along with my entire family, before Betsy and I were even allowed to be friends.

We double-dated all through high school, and we spent lots of our summer vacations together. By the time it was time for us to start thinking about college and our career options. We had already had numerous discussions and had shared our research.

Both of us were hoping that we would receive scholarships for academic achievements. Our grades were always above average despite some of our mischievous adventures.

My home's financial situation for me to be able to go to college was a little bit tougher because my parents had so many kids to pay for. My dad was a truck driver, and my mom worked at the local supermarket.

So, the summer before our senior year, we both decided that we would try to get good-paying jobs so that we could apply it towards our tuition for college. We racked our brains on what kind of job that would have to be. We lived in a bit of a remote area in North Carolina. But we thought there might be a possibility to stretch our search to some of the tourist destinations and work that summer waiting on tables for some big tips. Happy people would be happy tippers.

My mother had a sister who lived in one of those quaint, little tourist towns, so, as luck would have it, she helped us with our plans. We would be staying at my aunt's home, which was near some of the popular river rafting destinations, so there would be lots of happy vacationers who would be dining out and enjoying North Carolina's gorgeous rivers and mountains. To both of our surprise, Betsy's grandma said it was okay. We could not wait for summer to arrive. Our plan was that we would work hard and make some good money for school. But we also dreamed about meeting some good-looking guys and going to some great parties, too. This was going to be a summer to remember, and our last day of school was on June 6. Our summer vacation would start on June 7. Our lucky number and another sign that this was going to be our most amazing summer yet.

We went clothes shopping, which included some fabulous new shoes, too. We bought new bathing suits, and we were satisfied with our ensembles. We had high hopes about our chances of meeting some rich, smart, and good-looking guys. The guys would surely think, because of the way we were dressed and acted, that we were already college-age girls, guaranteeing that we were about having some fun.

That summer did not disappoint us. We made some good money waiting tables. We also met some great guys. We laughed and swam and enjoyed some amazing sunsets. Betsy met a guy named Duke, and it didn't take long before they started to become serious. I liked Duke, and I thought that he was good to Betsy. They spent a lot of time together. It was a little bit hard for me because before Duke came along, it was just the two of us doing everything together. But I had a few guys, too, and I could have gotten more serious if I had wanted to. But I stayed true to her as her best friend and was happy for her.

Duke's dad was a chiropractor, and his practice was close to the university where Betsy's grandmother worked. Her grandma knew Duke's dad. He had been in practice and the area for many years.

We were back at school, starting our senior year, and we had lots of stories to share with our friends at school, and likewise, they had summertime fun stories to share with us as well.

Duke mentioned to Betsy that her dad was looking for a part-time gal for after school to come in and help out in the office. This person who was needed would perform some light house-keeping duties, restocking, some office filing, and others. Duke told his dad that Betsy might be interested. His dad told Duke that since he knew her Grandmother and that Duke was dating her, he would be happy to go a little higher on the hourly wage to help with her college fund. Betsy had met both of Duke's parents, and by this time, she had been to their house for dinner on several occasions.

Duke's mom seemed a little snooty and a bit controlling, but we both wrote off that she would probably never approve of any girl who was dating her precious son. Duke could do no wrong in his mother's eyes. She kind of fawned all over him, and she loved to brag about him at every chance she got.

So, it was decided that Betsy would start working at Duke's father's office. She had her own car that her grandmother had already given her as a graduation gift. A nice car, too. She had a black convertible BMW with a sexy red leather interior. Riding with her in that car got both of us a lot of attention, horn honks, and whistles.

It seemed like our time together was getting to be less and less, with all the senior year obligations and then with Betsy working after school, too. And so, when we did have time to be together, we always had a lot to catch up on.

Betsy had been working at the office for about three months, when something she never expected happened. It was on a Friday, and she had something going on after school, so she was late getting to the office that day. I think it was just a little more than an hour later. So, because she went in late, she thought she would work an hour later to make up for it. Instead of leaving at 6:00 p.m., on that day, she worked until 7:00 p.m.. Nobody told her that she had to. She said she just knew that there were things that they counted on her handling, so she did not want to leave anything undone for somebody else to have to take care of.

This extra hour from between six and seven turned out to be a haunting mistake. Obviously, no one expected her to be there after 6:00 p.m. What she accidentally stumbled upon changed the course of her life and the plans that she had made.

At about 6:30 p.m. that night, as Betsy was coming up the stairs from the basement, she heard something. She had been getting supplies out of the stock room to replenish some of the supplies. When she got to the top of the stairs, she froze.

What she saw was Duke's father with a young teenage boy, and they were both naked from the waist down. She heard loud moaning and there was soft music playing. There was a light flickering, and she wasn't sure what that was. She wondered if they were possibly recording all of it. She said she panicked at what she was seeing. She told me that she froze in place for a minute, not knowing what to do. And then she decided to back herself back down the basement stairs. She said that one of the steps creaked, which terrified her that they might have heard it. Next, she said she decided to pretend that she had not seen or heard anything. From the bottom of the stairs, she called out, "Hello, is anyone still here? It's Betsy. I'll be all done down here in about ten minutes. Let me know if you need anything from the stockroom." She said she did her best to pretend that she knew nothing, and she got herself out of there the best she could that night.

Duke's father acted a little strange and uncomfortable trying to question her, wondering if she knew anything. Betsy said she knew that night that she had to quit working there, but she also said she knew she had to do it in a way that he would not suspect that she might know something.

Soon after, Betsy started sharing her plan with me. She planned to tell Duke and his parents that she feared her grades were starting to slip and that she would have to quit her after-school job. She thought this would work because they knew she needed scholarship money. But she also wanted to break it off with Duke. She knew she could no longer go to their house for dinner and act as if there was nothing wrong. She could not erase from her memory what she saw. Then, as if this wasn't bad enough, the next thing was strange things started to happen.

First, she thought that her phone was tapped, that she was

being tracked, and her computer was hacked. Then, she thought that she had been followed on a few occasions. One night, at her house, she thought that it looked like someone had been in her room and had been going through her desk and papers. I told her that I thought that she was just being paranoid. That she was imagining all of it. I kept telling her they wouldn't risk something like that. She kept telling me that they knew that they were at more risk if what happened ever got out and went public.

It kept getting worse. One day, she found out that Duke's mother had accused her of stealing from their cash drawer. She said that she had taken money numerous times, and some very large amounts of money. Betsy believed that they wanted to discredit her in any way that they could to make her look bad. To prove her untrustworthy in case she had seen something and might have possibly told someone else, which she did. She had told me. But again, I thought that some of what she was telling me was being blown out of proportion. However, I knew it was possible that they would want to hurt her and make her look bad. One day, she said she found a camera in her bedroom, as well as by her desk and computer. She told me she was being watched. I never saw the cameras myself, so again, I just wasn't sure. I thought she was overreacting.

She had been afraid to involve her grandmother at all. One reason was that she did not want to put her grandmother in danger. But she also did not want her to know because, with her grandmother being a law professor, Betsy knew her grandmother would not hesitate to contact the authorities. She knew this would be a huge scandal and one that would erupt into something very, very bad for everyone involved. She feared for both of their lives, too. After all, this was an important and prominent doctor in the community, and his wife was a philanthropist who chaired many clubs and ran in a lot of important social circles. Betsy said she knew there was no way they would let anyone destroy their reputation and everything that they had. Next, they started telling lies to their staff about Betsy. They were well prepared to protect themselves at any and at all costs.

The wife, on more than one occasion, tried to trick her and say things like, "You know you can be honest with me, and if you are, I will protect you."

This was making Betsy so stressed that she felt she was boxed into a corner, like a caged animal, and that her chance of surviving was not a possibility. When Betsy and Duke broke up, he started saying untrue things about her at school. His parents had to make her look bad to protect themselves, so they lied to Duke about her. And the strangest part about all this is that Duke's mother must have known all along about her husband's desires to have sex with other men. Betsy and I speculated that she probably looked the other way because she did not want to give up her rich and lavish lifestyle. Duke, at one time, said that his father made over four million dollars per year as a chiropractor, and he wanted Duke to take over his flourishing practice one day. If the truth came out, a lot of lives would be ruined.

I started seeing Betsy less and less. She was isolating herself, and she was hurt that I was not believing everything that she was telling me. I feel bad about this, but it just seemed so crazy and desperate. I believed what she said she saw happen. I just could not completely believe all the tracking, hacking, and following her. What I know now is that it was all true. Every bit of it.

I was her best friend, and I thought I knew better. I thought her behavior was because she was having a nervous breakdown. I missed it. I let her down. But I couldn't have changed any of the course of events that took place.

It had been thirteen years since Betsy's parents were killed in the tragic car accident. On August 7, in the same month and on the same day that they died, Betsy took her life. The note that she left simply said, "I am sorry. Please forgive me. I want to be with my mother and father in heaven and at peace. Goodbye to my beautiful and loving grandmother and to my best friend Abbey. Please know that you were the best friend that anyone could ever hope for."

Months after Betsy died, a story appeared on the local news one evening. A young man came forward and accused the doctor of using him for sex. He also accused the doctor and his wife of trying to destroy his reputation in order to protect themselves. He went on to say that he wished that he had come forward sooner because if he had, it might have helped others. I wondered if it was possible that he had seen Betsy on the stairs that night at the doctor's office. I wondered if it was the same guy.

My purpose and intent are to make her tragedy known but without hurting anyone else. My reasons are pure. There could be a time in your life when you might know someone who is filled with fear and desperation. Don't be so quick to dismiss what they are telling you. Don't be so quick to think that you know what is really going on. Don't be so quick to judge. Bad things happen. I must admit that I was naïve at that time. I am older now, and I hear and read about some of the awful things that go on in this world.

I could not have changed the course of what happened, but I know I added to her desperation by doubting some of it. I wasn't there, and I wasn't seeing it, so I should not have been the judge and jury on any of it. She was desperate and scared, and for all the right reasons.

Currently, I am a grief counselor at my church. My friend Betsy has helped me to become a better listener and a more compassionate person. Because of her, I am helping many people. You need to have courage, stay hopeful, and have faith, even at the times in your life when you think God is not listening. When you think no one cares.

Betsy left a note for me on the day that she took her life. To commemorate her, on August 7 of every year I do a balloon release to the heavens. The balloon contains a folded paper note with a special message from me to her. I want her to know how blessed I was to have her in my life.

I feel like she is still sitting next to me on the bus. It comforts me and guides me.

A Letter from My Cousin

Sorry I've taken so long to get back to you. Not making excuses but it seems like I can't stay caught up. I found out the best thing about winter is I get a break for a few months, lol. It was such a blessing to see you. Just hate the short visits, but still very thankful for them. I wish I could tell you in words how much you mean to me. I just haven't been able to know how to tell you. I'm not sure how God managed to bring us together. I mean, we've always been family, but for so many years we didn't even talk and here we are anxiously awaiting the next visit. It's just simply amazing to me. All the years that passed, I never knew what was yet to be. And then because of a "*book*," it started a whole new chapter. Although there was a lot of pain and heartache, you'll never understand the impact it's made for me. I can only talk for me and to read in words what my life was like and not just hearing it, reading it, but finally getting to feel it, to capture those moments in my life that were kept hidden and the struggle that was always there to try to keep my mind from being occupied by those thoughts, the fear, the pain and heartaches and so many more things that my old feeble mind wanted to just erase and start all over. To have someone *finally* believe in me but also four others, too, is almost more than I ever in my lifetime thought would happen.

For a period of time, I wanted to just give up on everything and come to terms that life wasn't how I heard it was or that my thoughts would never become a reality; little did I know that God was much bigger than anything I knew. He had already laid out a plan for me and allowed me to find that path. Struggles? Oh, most definitely, it wasn't an easy road. I started having different kinds of thoughts and my dreams were brighter than ever. But I didn't do it by myself. First, it was God: He was always there when I started to question, give up, make decisions, and in every way, every situation, struggle, heartache, or anything and everything I felt. He, my Lord, gave me the answers. Couldn't be more thankful to Him for all He's done for me. I always, *always* prayed He would keep and protect all of us. Take us away from the chains that had us bound. You said that I pretty much paid for what I have, not with money but with sacrifices. If you only knew how powerfully that hit me. As I said before, God's given me such a wonderful gift that words can't describe. Yep, I'm talking about you. The impact you've made on my life is unreal. You listen, you cry, hurt, laugh, suggest, but never, and I mean *never*, have you ever once turned away from me or any of us. You have done nothing but give us hope, love, care, kindness, compassion, and, oh goodness, so much more. And it's been from the heart. It's been true and real and heartfelt. I haven't had a whole lot of that kind of experience in my lifetime. People have tried, but it never made an impact on me like this, like I imagined it should've been. I could probably count, if I had to, the ones who I could truly say have been true, caring people in my life.

As I've gotten older, I know and realize how strong the word "love" is. I've learned *what* love really is. It's certainly been an experience, an eye-opener, and I try really hard to make sure I let those that I care about and love with that kind of love know how I feel. I can't let it go and not tell you. I told you before you left that you have my heart, and I truly mean that. I know you've struggled some of those same ways and even more in other ways, and maybe that's God's way to give us that bond we now have. If we looked back in time and how we *all* suffered to just have what we have now, I know, for me, I would've never thought it possible. But as we walked down this path, we were so graciously given we had this time to share our lives. I hope to make as many memories as I can. I sometimes tell people I have this memory vault, and what's locked inside is worth more to me than any money, diamonds, or gold could buy. It's all been bought and paid for and in safe keeping now. It still has room for a bunch more, so I'm ready to continue building, hoping, and filling it up! So how do I say "thank you" for all that? I've never figured that out yet. All I know is to do my best and give that same kind of love in return. I know it'll never get paid, but I'm sure gonna keep trying. Momma always told me, "Never stop, never give up on something your heart desires." All I've ever really wanted in life was for my brothers and sisters to have nothing but goodness, peace, prosperity, and love. As for myself, well, those same things, along with a happy home that's filled with love as I always thought it should be. To live long enough to see my siblings away from the life we had. But for me, I hoped my life and my heart would never reflect on the things I suffered with and that I would have a light to shine for others. That somehow, some way, I could never allow those "things" to let others see what I had endured as a child. That they would only know if I chose to tell. That not many would know the "real" me.

God surely has blessed me and answered my prayers. He's given above my imagination. Again, I'm sorry this is so long, but I had to tell you; I had to let you know how thankful I am for you. How blessed God has given us this bond and to let us find each other the way He has. "Thank you" isn't enough to begin with, but all I can do is keep trying. I *thank you* from the very depth of my heart, soul, and mind. To say "I love you" is mild compared to how I feel. Just always know you have my heart. Can't wait till next visit. Love you *big*!!!

POSTSCRIPT

RITA, COUNSELOR, INTERVIEW AND STORY.

Sharon says, "It has happened to me one too many times, so now I feel safer staying under the radar. I feel safer staying under the radar. I can't take a chance with you. I dare not trust you." This is how she feels about most people whom she meets. "You won't find me on social media. I lay low, off the grid, and under the radar."

At the onset, with her wanting to stay under the radar, one might think that she might be a bit paranoid. But my experience over many years in therapy discussions is that this is typically a person who has been burnt by someone else just one too many times. They trusted, they shared private details about themselves, given money, nice gifts, and more, only to find out that what they thought was a genuine friendship or working relationship or a wonderful spouse was not that at all. They were being used to benefit the other person no matter what the cost. They were being lied to over and over again. It did not matter to the perpetrator how low they had to go to get what they wanted. And then, when they did get what they wanted, it still wasn't enough. It did not stop there. The perpetrator then, to keep themselves from looking bad, had to finish off their victim by destroying their reputation. Lies would be told, and over-exaggerations would be made by the perpetrator to make the other person look bad. The perpetrator might have used what is referred to many times as flying monkeys, social media, and any sources to make themselves look good and to make their victim the bad guy. In the meantime, the perpetrator, the real bad guy, his or her wealth continued to grow, they took more vacations, enjoyed nice dinners, and lived in nice houses. People thought they were successful, and they were admired. For many, it would feel like "the bad guy wins again!"

Beware because these untruthful and phony do-gooders wear a mask, and they are not always easy to spot.

Their mask might look like this, which is why it throws others off track. Their son is in Eagle Scouts, at the highest of levels, they volunteer for everything at church and at school, they talk about religion all the time, they donate to numerous charities, they post on social media all the wonderful and great things that they say and do. Always promoting themselves. They are successful in their work, and sometimes, it is because they have taken advantage of others to get where they are. They put themselves and their needs and wants before others. Sometimes, their smile is not even real. But you miss that, too, but not before it is too late.

Keeping some distance helps to protect yourself. The more that others know about you, the more it can be used against you by someone who has bad intentions.

Some people have no conscience. They don't even try to justify their evil ways. It works for them and gets them what they want regardless of who it may hurt. It is their *modus operandi.*

Many people are on the same hamster wheel of believing the best in others only to find out that they got it completely wrong.

Truly, there are many good people in this world. And some of those good people will have nice houses, take vacations, and have good jobs, too. *There are good guys and bad guys, and sometimes, it is hard to tell the difference.* So, as we work through this, instead of isolating one's self—just don't be so quick and accepting to start a friendship, loan money, or share something personal. Because the person you thought you knew might not be who the person really is or someone who has good intentions.

Take back your power! Don't be so eager to open your door and become fast friends or make excuses for an unhealthy relationship. You deserve to be treated with respect. Set boundaries, lay low when you feel you need to, and test the waters before diving in. Don't make the same mistakes over and over again. Cut the people out of your life who are unhealthy for you. You have the power to say "no." Respect yourself. You know your intentions are good, regardless of what others may be saying about you or doing behind your back. Let God be your vindicator because evil is hard to fight on your own. Especially when the mask that the bad guy is wearing is such a great disguise. And pray for your enemies and those who have wronged you.

As it says in Matthew 5:43–44 (NIV), "You have heard that it was said, 'Love your neighbor and hate your enemy.' *But I tell you, love your enemies and pray for those who persecute you.*"

Bibliography

Bedlack, Richard. n.d. *ALSUntangled*. https://www.alsuntangled.
com/

Biggers, Larissa. 2022. "9 Signs of Narcissistic Personality Disorder." *Duke Health*. December 15, 2022. https://www.
dukehealth.org/blog/9-signs-of-narcissistic-personality-disor-
der

Cherry, Kim. n.d. *ALS Winners – The Road To Recovery*. Accessed March 22, 2024. https://www.alswinners.com/

Chimaobi Kalu, Micheal. 2019. "Vietnam Vermin: The Story of
the Tunnel Rats." *War History Online*. March 23, 2019.
https://www.warhistoryonline.com/instant-articles/tunnel-
rats-of-the-vietnam-war.html

Kairos Prison Ministry International. n.d. "The Impact Of Kairos Prison Ministry." *Kairos Prison Ministry*. Accessed
March 22, 2024. https://kairosprisonministry.org/im-
pact-of-kairos-prison-ministry/

Mackenzie, Jackson. 2015. *Psychopath Free: Recovering from
Emotionally Abusive Relationships With Narcissists, Sociopaths, and Other Toxic People*. Berkley; Expanded
edition.

Nannestad, Chloë. 2024. "Why Four-Leaf Clovers Are Considered Lucky." Reader's Digest. March 21, 2024. https://www.rd.com/article/four-leaf-clover/

The Lacasa Center. Accessed March 22, 2024. https://lacasacenter.org/

Valentine, Tricia S. 1995. Don't Call Us Orphans: An Oral History of the Jr. Order of United American Mechanics National Orphans' Home. Tiffin, Ohio: Virgin Alley Press.

Van Zyl, Llewellyn E. 2023. "Stockholm Syndrome: Why Some People Bond with Abusive Partners." *Psychology Today*. August 14, 2023. https://www.psychologytoday.com/nz/blog/happybytes/202308/stockholm-syndrome-why-some-people-bond-with-abusive-partners

Women In Distress. Accessed March 22, 2024. https://widbroward.org/

RESOURCES

Women in Distress of Broward County, Inc. (WID) is a full-service domestic violence center located in Broward County, Florida. WID offers a variety of programs for survivors, including a 140-bed emergency shelter for those fleeing. In addition, WID has a pet shelter so survivors with pets can take their animals with them and be assured the abuser will not harm the animal.

WID also has a full therapeutic team with a variety of interventions, including equine therapy for children, art therapy, sand tray, and play therapy, as well as EMDR and many others. On the campus, there is a childcare center and a full outreach office with the same services offered as the residential setting (housing advocacy, financial literacy, and resource guidance).

WID will hit fifty years, and while this is a wonderful business milestone, it is a chilling reminder of how much WID has to grow to meet the continual and complicated needs of domestic violence victims and a sobering reminder that violence against others is a true community problem.

24-Hour Crisis Hotline: 954.761.1133

Website: https://widbroward.org/

Alcoholics Anonymous. aa.org

National Domestic Violence Hotline: 1-800-799-7233 (SAFE) or 1-800-787-3224

Substance Abuse and Mental Health Services Administration: https://www.samhsa.gov/ Toll-free hotline: 1-800-662-HELP (4357)

Childhelp National Child Abuse Hotline: 1-800-422-4453

Printed in the USA
CPSIA information can be obtained
at www.ICGtesting.com
JSHW011148081024
71062JS00001B/4